THE CHRIST IN MY CANCER

Finding the Peace of Christ Amidst the Firestorms of Life

DR. SCOTT E. DAVIS

CLAY BRIDGES
P R E S S

The Christ in My Cancer

Copyright © 2023 by Dr. Scott E. Davis

Published by Clay Bridges Press in Houston, TX
www.Claybridgespress.com

All rights reserved. No part of this publication may be reproduced, stored in a retrieval system, or transmitted in any form by any means, electronic, mechanical, photocopy, recording, or otherwise, without the prior permission of the publisher, except as provided for by USA copyright law.

Scripture quotations marked (ESV) are taken from the ESV® Bible (The Holy Bible, English Standard Version®), copyright © 2001 by Crossway, a publishing ministry of Good News Publishers. Used by permission. All rights reserved.

eISBN: 978-1-68488-052-2
ISBN: 978-1-68488-051-5

Special Sales: Most Lucid Books titles are available in special quantity discounts. Custom imprinting or excerpting can also be done to fit special needs. Contact Lucid Books at info@claybridgespress.com

In loving memory of my husband.

Scott Davis
May 6, 1962 - November 19, 2022

To my Family and Friends:

I need to take time to acknowledge my family, children, and many friends who have shown great support, meals on a regular basis, and a great many prayers on our behalf. I also need to acknowledge my videographer who regularly edits the videos that we produce online. She truly does an amazing job and takes the time out of her work week to publish them—it is my hope and prayer that Jesus would use these videos to His Glory.

Through this journey, I have learned one thing very clearly. The Bride of Christ is astounding in His Glory, and He uses her to provide such remarkable grace and mercy.

So many people have reached out in prayer and support. We are truly blessed beyond anything that I deserve. People have provided food for us almost every other day since coming home from Pittsburgh. Enough so that we have had such a bounty that there is rarely a need to provide dinners for ourselves (leftovers have been delicious and abundant).

My children and their spouses are, as always, my heroes and are always there to help. I love you guys more than you may ever know. I also have the most adorable grandchildren I could ever imagine—I am indeed blessed by family.

My wife is a gift from God Himself, and it is my solemn prayer that He will mold me into the husband that she deserves. (For many years I have not been that husband and she certainly deserves more than I can ever provide.)

Thank you all and be blessed in His grace and mercy as I have been. As a very good friend just told me—God already has healed me, He just hasn't cured me!

- Scott Davis

Take a few moments and contemplate the words
of this magnificent hymn.

Amazing Grace

Written by English Poet John Newton in 1772 and published in 1779

Amazing Grace, how sweet the sound
That saved a wretch like me
I once was lost, but now am found
Was blind but now I see
Was Grace that taught my heart to fear
And Grace, my fears relieved
How precious did that Grace appear
The hour I first believed
Through many dangers, toils, and snares
We have already come
'Twas Grace that brought us safe thus far
And Grace will lead us home
And Grace will lead us home
Amazing Grace, how sweet the sound
That saved a wretch like me
I once was lost but now am found
Was blind, but now I see
Was blind, but now I see

TABLE OF CONTENTS

Preface ix

Introduction 1

Part 1: The Faith Relationship with Jesus Christ 9

    Chapter 1: Suffering and the Disciple of Christ 11

    Chapter 2: Peace Amidst the Storm 27

    Chapter 3: The Hope and Humility of Jesus Christ 43

    Chapter 4: The Wide and Narrow Gates 55

    Chapter 5: The Christian Life on the Hard Road 69

    Chapter 6: Guilt, Grace, and Gratitude 85

    Chapter 7: Faith 95

    Chapter 8: Discipleship: 107

Part 2: The Armor of God 111

    Chapter 9: A Call to Arms 113

    Chapter 10: How Big is Your God? 127

    Chapter 11: The Belt of Truth 141

    Chapter 12: The Breastplate of Righteousness 151

    Chapter 13: The Gospel of Peace 163

    Chapter 14: The Shield of Faith 175

    Chapter 15: The Helmet of Salvation 189

    Chapter 16: The Sword of the Spirit 203

    Chapter 17: Prayer 217

PREFACE

Into the Inferno

Most of us have read the opening chapters of the book of Job as a salve to heal the pain and hurt that comes from the sin and pain of this world that so besets us, but few read beyond these to see the interaction between God and Job as the chapter comes to a close. Much like me, Job had become arrogant and prideful of his faith relationship with God, failing as I did to remember one critical piece of Scripture.

In Job 24-37, we read that Elihu presents two different pictures of our response to God in our trials, one of our own wisdom or the wisdom of the fear of God. On February 23rd, 2022 I experienced a grand mal seizure and was diagnosed with three incurable brain tumors called Glioblastoma, for which brain surgery to remove the largest was required. I literally woke up on a surgical gurney with a large man in a white lab coat drawing a sharpie-line on my forehead as he marked out the lines in my skull through which he planned to remove the tumor.

Job had, as had I, fallen under the delusion of his own wisdom. During the remaining chapters of the book, God proceeds to show Job the ignorance of his pride . . .

God is a God of Love, yes, and we need to remember that and proclaim it as His disciples, but He is also an angry God who is NOT to be trifled with. Deuteronomy 9:8 reminds us, "Even at Horeb you provoked the Lord to wrath, and the Lord was so angry with you that he was ready to destroy you." Job and indeed I needed to be very careful not to endure that wrath.

The Christ in my Cancer

God's response to Job was clear:
God created and Job was not involved,
God Judges and Job is not involved,
God ordains with no input from Job,
God allows with zero input from Job.

I, like Job, had become all these things and drew the wrath of Creator God and foolishly spoke to God in a way that invoked a swift and severe response. We all face firestorms in our lives, but it is how we as Disciples respond to those events that should differentiate us from the world in which we are bound. Do we want healing from our pain and hurt, or do we simply seek His grace and peace in it? Many of us follow the former path, but God in His magnificent grace and mercy has shown me incredible peace and for that, I am incredibly blessed.

This is the story of Christ's testimony; it is not mine and it was written for me from before time began—how can I possibly be anything but humbly blessed through it? I am now in the company of great men of God that He has brought low and I have been given the message of hope that only Jesus Christ can offer.

Over the past two weeks, He has allowed me to experience His grace and mercy through His children, and as my son told someone yesterday, "This is the most traumatic event our family has ever experienced, and he is more at peace than I have seen him in years."

The following Tuesday morning, March 1st, I was given Gamma Knife radiation which is designed to pinpoint the remaining tumors and shrink them into submission and told I could go home for follow-up appointments with local doctors at Lehigh Valley Hospital in Allentown, PA.

Monday, March 7th, was a rough day, hearing words like Glioblastoma (an incurable brain cancer) that may be put into remission but will never go away. Words like chemotherapy, radiation therapy, etc. We went for a bucket of KFC on the way home.

I have no idea how much prayer has been sent to God on my behalf, but I accept it all and the prayers must have been heard, because

Preface

following lots of my own prayers, He brought me to understand a few things I needed to know.

I do indeed have an expiration date (as we all do—only now do I understand that fact more clearly than ever before, indeed more than many who will hear or read this). Every day until that expiration date from here on out is a bonus day to be used for His glory and His purposes only and can never be wasted. I, for the first time in my life, need to take time for myself and away from the business that I have spent years building, time for my cancer care, time for my dear wife and children, and most importantly time for Jesus Christ, time to pursue the chief end of man as found in the Westminster Shorter Catechism.

I have become the loudest spokesperson for His Glory lately and do not care what others may think of me. Man's chief end is to glorify God and to enjoy him forever. Take a few moments to look up a few of these amazing scriptures that showcase God's glory: Ps. 86:9; Isa. 60:21; Rom. 11:36; 1 Cor. 6:20; 10:31; Rev. 4:11 Ps. 16:5-11; 144:15; Isa. 12:2; Luke 2:10; Phil. 4:4; Rev. 21:3-4.

I am looking at a long road in this—six- and one-half weeks of Radiation and Chemotherapy followed by a 4-week break and then Chemotherapy 3 to 4 days per week for maintenance and constant MRIs to keep an eye on future growth, reduction of the 2 remaining tumors. I am told that this cancer is not curable and the best I can hope for is remission, I tell them that my Hope is in Christ, my plan is for remission and my prayer is that whether through my life or eventual death my purpose is His—to lift Him as high onto the highest hill I can find and glorify His name with every breath I have left in me. And yes—I am at peace in a way that can ONLY be provided by His Holy Spirit.

I understand that there will be those indeed who want God to physically heal me through this, and yes—He is the creator God and can indeed do anything He pleases, but it has been my experience through Scripture that once God places one of His into this inferno, He generally does not place them back into the sin-soaked world that they have come to hate but calls them home to the reward He has waiting for them. How amazingly glorious that will be. Jesus Christ, my dad, Pop-Pop, and 100-day-old grandson Colton Davis will be there to greet me. (And now I am tearing up—it happens a lot these days). I will have no questions for Him upon my arrival, no interest in rewards or streets paved with gold. The greatest of my desires is to simply sit at His feet and enjoy Him for He is my Christ, my Messiah, my hope, my healer, my God, and my King!

That being said, I no longer think about remission or recovery for my own sake, because my desire to serve Him is so great. After having done some research, the new plan is this—I have begun a full Keto diet intending to deprive and starve the cancer of the sugars upon which it thrives. This book and subsequent videos and blog posts tracking this journey are intended to provide the details of this great gift I have been given, highlighting His handiwork in and through it to show the world, that we can indeed survive the massive firestorms that we find ourselves in while finding the peace that is beyond all understanding, The hope that is found in Christ, and the happiness that comes from enjoying Him forever.

Whatever the ultimate outcome of this earthly piece of flesh, this book will end when my flesh does. I pray it offers the hope that I am experiencing, the peace that gives rest, and joy to those also in need. Once more, I think of what a good friend reminded me recently, I have been healed, I just haven't been cured yet.

May the God of magnificent grace and mercy guard you and keep you as you walk through the firestorms of your own life and may He give you a glimpse of the wondrous nature of His love.

I promise you—there can be peace in your life even though the worst storms imaginable may be rolling through your life at this very moment.

> Blessed be the God and Father of our Lord Jesus Christ! According to his great mercy, he has caused us to be born again to a living hope through the resurrection of Jesus Christ from the dead, to an inheritance that is imperishable, undefiled, and unfading, kept in heaven for

Preface

you, who by God's power are being guarded through faith for a salvation ready to be revealed in the last time. In this you rejoice, though now for a little while, if necessary, you have been grieved by various trials, so that the tested genuineness of your faith—more precious than gold that perishes though it is tested by fire—may be found to result in praise and glory and honor at the revelation of Jesus Christ. Though you have not seen him, you love him. Though you do not now see him, you believe in him and rejoice with joy that is inexpressible and filled with glory, obtaining the outcome of your faith, the salvation of your souls.

Concerning this salvation, the prophets who prophesied about the grace that was to be yours searched and inquired carefully, inquiring what person or time[a] the Spirit of Christ in them was indicating when he predicted the sufferings of Christ and the subsequent glories. It was revealed to them that they were serving not themselves but you, in the things that have now been announced to you through those who preached the good news to you by the Holy Spirit sent from heaven, things into which angels long to look.

Therefore, preparing your minds for action,[b] and being sober-minded, set your hope fully on the grace that will be brought to you at the revelation of Jesus Christ. As obedient children, do not be conformed to the passions of your former ignorance, but as he who called you is holy, you also be holy in all your conduct, since it is written, "You shall be holy, for I am holy." And if you call on him as Father who judges impartially according to each one's deeds, conduct yourselves with fear throughout the time of your exile.

1 Peter 1: 3-17

INTRODUCTION

All Authority

There was a time in my life when I did a lot of sailing with a good friend of mine who I knew from work. Unfortunately, he passed from cancer in 2009 and I still miss him greatly. During the years in which we were friends, he taught me a great deal about the art of sailing. I could be a slow study at times as he quietly and patiently taught me to properly helm the vessel (boat). The problem was that I tended to constantly bounce from side to side much like driving a car between the left and the right lanes of traffic. It was during one of these trips that he gave me a sage piece of advice which helped tremendously and today gives me the assurance and strength to now carry on and take heed. The lesson learned—to set my course to Jesus Christ and Him alone as I focus all of my efforts on holding a single point on the horizon, as He stands on the horizon and calls me home. And when I can stay focused, my purpose clears and my course steadies. We will all go through the various storms that we find at sea as we go through this life—this book is written to provide comfort when comfort is needed, rest when rest is required, faith when faith is lacking, and strength when our own strength fails us.

In all that has transpired over the past few months with my cancer, radiation, and chemo I have found that once again I have needed to set my course to a single point on the horizon (Jesus Christ, King of Kings, and Lord of Lords) and I find it divinely comforting to dwell on Him while in midst of this storm.

That is the purpose of this book—to put on full display the character and person of Jesus Christ. For His purposes and to His glory— For after all "He has been given ALL Authority in Heaven and on earth."

The Christ in my Cancer

> And you were dead in the trespasses and sins in which you once walked, following the course of this world, following the prince of the power of the air, the spirit that is now at work in the sons of disobedience—among whom we all once lived in the passions of our flesh, carrying out the desires of the body and the mind, and were by nature children of wrath, like the rest of mankind. But God, being rich in mercy, because of the great love with which he loved us, even when we were dead in our trespasses, made us alive together with Christ—by grace, you have been saved—and raised us up with him and seated us with him in the heavenly places in Christ Jesus, so that in the coming ages he might show the immeasurable riches of his grace in kindness toward us in Christ Jesus. For by grace, you have been saved through faith. And this is not your own doing; it is the gift of God, not a result of works, so that no one may boast. For we are his workmanship, created in Christ Jesus for good works, which God prepared beforehand, that we should walk in them.
>
> Ephesians 2:1-10.

I became critical of those I referred to as nameplate Christians; those who went to church on Sunday mornings with a nameplate on their lapels that read "Christian" in which they sit with a holiness that bespoke their theology and then they would go back into work on Monday mornings without the "Christian" lapel pins as they settle far too easily into their workday lives, generally leaving their Christian walk behind as they entered into the desires and enticements of the world and careers in which they found themselves, to seek gain in a sin-soaked world ruled by the enemy of our souls.

> For the time is coming when people will not endure sound teaching but having itching ears they will accumulate for themselves teachers to suit their own passions, will turn away from listening to the truth, and wander off

Introduction

into myths. As for you, always be sober-minded, endure suffering, do the work of an evangelist, and fulfill your ministry.

2 Timothy 4:3-5

O God, you are my God; earnestly I seek you; my soul thirsts for you; my flesh faints for you, as in a dry and weary land where there is no water. So, I have looked upon you in the sanctuary, beholding your power and glory. Because your steadfast love is better than life, my lips will praise you. So, I will bless you as long as I live; in your name I will lift up my hands. My soul will be satisfied as with fat and rich food, and my mouth praise you with joyful lips, when I remember you upon my bed, and meditate on you in the watches of the night; for you have been my help, and in the shadow of your wings I will sing for joy. My soul clings to you; your right hand upholds me.

Psalm 63:1-8

The Journey Begins

And it begins with 3 of the most important tools at my disposal. Specifically in this order . . .

My Faith (which has grown 10,000 percent in the past 2 weeks)

My family (who has been incredibly wonderful through all of this)

My friends and Christian brothers and sisters—(Who have provided meals, companionship, and prayers throughout—people who are now more valuable to me than all of the gold and silver in the world)

Monday, March 14th, 2022: MRI to determine the decrease or growth of the 2 remaining tumors. Apparently, the Doctors were pleased with the results as we are now moving on to the treatment phase at the end of the month. Interesting that they asked me when I went in for the MRI if I had ever had one before to which I answered "yes" of course—They had done several while I was in Pittsburgh—After I was done, I told them this time was very noisy, but that might be because I was in a medically induced coma for the first one.

Tuesday, March 15th, 2022: Follow-up with radiation doctor to be fit for a mask and set the plan for my treatments. This took about 30 minutes after which they briefly discussed the plan. 30 minutes on a very hard table—otherwise this was not as bad as I had thought.

Monday, March 21st, 2022: Appointment with Chemo Doctor... Several hours at the hospital to review treatments and education on Chemo, etc. They told me that the MRI looks really good—the tumors are not growing (great news overall).

Monday, March 28th, 2022: Treatments begin...

In short, I am at a better place in my life at this moment than I have been in many years. The grace and mercy of God Almighty have washed over me in a way that I have never experienced before. I have no fear anymore... No fear of death because I have already been dead through this. No fear of ridicule either. As anyone who has ever evangelized about Jesus Christ will certainly know the trepidation that comes with that (none of us really wants to be ridiculed for our faith) and I have always found it somewhat scary to do so as many people do indeed mock us for our faith when we speak of it. Truly, that fear is fully gone now. I am FREE and it is amazing. I might even say that this whole brain tumor thing is a GREAT blessing because I would have never been able to experience this freedom in Christ without it. Crazy, right? By the world's standards, yes, it is indeed crazy—and that is what makes this so very special. None of it applies to the world's standards, but to God's standards.

The doctors continue to look at me as if they are giving me a death sentence and I need to help them understand that I DO NOT have a death sentence in this—I have a life sentence instead. I have been sentenced to abundant life in all of this. I do not know how many bonus days or hours I have left, but I now have a brand-new life, raised from the dead in Christ, with freedom and joy that I have never experienced before, and in many ways, I am truly excited to embark on this new life. I now have the freedom to live as Christ lived, needing to be more compassionate with

Introduction

others than I have been in the past, less demanding than ever before, and more Christlike than ever before. I will one day meet my Savior and need to spend the time He has just given me in His service. As a good friend recently told me, "You will meet Jesus, it might be time to learn as much about Him now as He lets you."

Following a recent MRI and after the radiation and Chemo treatments for 6 weeks, my Oncologist said, "I see some things I don't like." Apparently, the 2 tumors in the back of my brain are not shrinking but perhaps growing. It would also seem that there is a third tumor they want to stay on top of. For now, I am getting a double dose of chemo for 5 days out of each month. So far the nausea has been fine, though when the doctor said it might constipate me, she wasn't kidding! Still trying to maintain the KETO diet to starve the cancer, but it's tough some days. Who am I kidding? There are a lot of rough days recently. I now wonder most nights when I go to bed if He will be gracious enough to allow me to wake again the next morning.

Death unto Life

As Christians, we often use terms like Death to Self, Born Again, or Risen in Christ, but I think most of us have this wrong. Much as I have done throughout my life, I said the same words and behaved as if the World was all that existed. I lived for career and success (the world's standard of success, anyway). In Galatians 3:20, the apostle Paul sums it up best for us,

> I have been crucified with Christ. It is no longer I who live, but Christ who lives in me. And the life I now live in the flesh I live by faith in the Son of God, who loved me and gave himself for me.
>
> Galatians 3:20

For truly thanks to His grace and great mercy, and through cancer, I have indeed now died to the world and risen to a new life in Christ. Something is enlightening about this revelation and it tends to change one's perspective on things.

I no longer have any desire for the things which I was once driven by, and now have the great pleasure to step into a brand-new life each day and am truly excited about this new life. His grace and mercy pour over me each day and I am blessed to be able to step out each day into His light and majesty. Every single day, I now wake up and thank Him for the privilege and blessing of it.

Dumbest Things to Say to God Almighty

I have said every single one of them. Never, ever pray for patience because God will not give you patience, but opportunities to be patient. Never, ever pray for humility because God will not give you humility, but opportunities to be humble. And most importantly, never, ever press God on His will because He will squash you like a bug on a windshield as He did with me.

March 22nd, 2022: If you remember I had asked Him to find me either a pew or a pulpit. He found me a pew that I am absolutely delighted to sit in. This past Sunday, we had lunch and broke bread with the pastor and his wife after church. I believe here is a man who has a true love of those whom he has been called to shepherd and has no interest in agendas or standing behind a denominational doctrine. My prayer is that God would continue to soften his heart and bless his ministry and family.

I am so very excited as to where this new life I have been given is going for me. I feel like I have spent the past 60 years slogging around in the excrement of human sin and now have a chance at a brand new, beautiful, clean, fresh life that I get to experience every single Bonus Day I have left. We all know we are going to die one day, but how many of us realize that and do something of value with those days we have left for Him in the time we have on this earth? Many, I fear, have no idea of the nature of those remaining days as they traverse their lives under the weight of bills, status, careers, etc.

We travel the remainder of our lives, filling the void within with all the stuff we can find in the world around us. It can and should be different. I see everything through clear eyes now, no longer are my eyes covered

Introduction

by rose-colored glasses, seeing darkly through a veil, but I now see everything so very clearly, I hear the world now from a new perspective. Everything smells cleaner, and food tastes better. People are more loving and beautiful in my eyes. Jesus Christ is so very good, and I am blessed beyond my wildest imagination to have been given this experience.

In truth, I am in very good company. Paul Washer and Voddie Baucham, two men whom I respect greatly as men of great Godly character, have in recent years been struck with difficult health problems. I know and see what God has done through the ministry of these 2 men. I simply have terminal brain cancer and truly can't wait to see what Jesus might have in store for me as I move through this brand-new life in Christ. GLORIOUS.

Even more importantly, He has now made it very clear what my job is and is not. My job IS NOT to correct or interfere in the faith relationship of those who call on His name, that is Christ's job. Mine is to simply find the tallest hill I can stand on and proclaim the glories of His grace and gospel. In that light, I will be restoring the Grey Matters Media Rumble page and doing what I should have known before I pushed a Holy God into a corner and demanded He answers me.

I will sit in a pew under the teaching of a God-fearing pastor and use every resource available to proclaim His name—regardless of the cost. Seem I have already died and been brought back to life. I have nothing to fear. I need to get the t-shirt "Death—been there, done that, got the t-shirt" which likely makes me the freest man you know.

PART 1

The Faith Relationship with Jesus Christ

CHAPTER 1

Suffering and the Disciple of Christ

June 3rd, 2022:

Had a follow-up appointment with my Oncologist yesterday to review my latest MRI results, etc. Unfortunately, the 2 tumors in the rear of my brain do not seem to be shrinking, but on the contrary, are growing, and there seems to now be a third that they want to keep their eyes on. Life is starting to get harder—Needing prayers. We are planning to spend a short week at home and then off to Ocean City, New Jersey— and I can't wait—LOVE that place. 7 days at a beautiful beach condo with my wife. All courtesy of the "A Week Away" Foundation. Amazing trip—thank you, guys!

Scott

Hard pressed but not crushed

> We are afflicted in every way, but not crushed; perplexed, but not driven to despair; persecuted, but not forsaken; struck down, but not destroyed; always carrying in the body the death of Jesus, so that the life of Jesus may also be manifested in our bodies.
>
> 2 Corinthians 4:8-10

The Christ in my Cancer

Paul tells us that, as Christians, we are 'afflicted in every way, but are not crushed'. Afflicted in every way is much to the contrary of many Western Christian Movements today that promise prosperity. Clearly, the Apostle Paul had a different idea of the Christian Life. Pain and suffering are to be expected as a natural part of a life lived for Christ. And while we will indeed experience great suffering in this life, we will not be crushed or destroyed by it. We are covered in the grace and mercy of Jesus Christ as He lives in us and makes Himself known to us as He manifests in us through these difficult times. It is this life in Christ that provides for true and lasting peace amidst the storms.

Every single one of us realizes we indeed have an expiration date. For most, it is an unknown date that we tend to put in the back of our minds and forget. The only real question to be asked is this—what will you do with the days you yet have remaining? As for me, I will stand on the highest hill I can find and raise Jesus Christ up and proclaim him with every remaining breath I have because He is indeed worthy.

When you reach the end of your rope, what do you think God might do? He generally seems to make your rope longer, because it is in His strength that we can hold on or stand as it tells us to do in Ephesians 6.

> Now the eleven disciples went to Galilee, to the mountain to which Jesus had directed them. And when they saw Him, they worshiped Him, but some doubted. And Jesus came and said to them "All authority in heaven and on earth has been given to me."
>
> Matthew 28:16-18

Jesus is telling us that it is HE who is in charge. He says that ALL Authority in Heaven AND on Earth has been given to Him by the Father. Everywhere and everything is under His complete control. What great comfort for those who are standing in Him! Nothing on this earth or in my body can alter the course He has set for me in this journey and if He has set the course then what have I to be concerned about? He just makes my rope longer and then gives me the strength to hold it even tighter. It is His and His alone. I have NO part in the matter. Actually, I can change my diet, go to every treatment, and take all the chemo they prescribe, but in the end, it makes no difference—I will live the number of days Jesus Christ has allotted me.

The point is this—Jesus will never give us more weight than we think we can carry but will always give the weight He knows we CAN carry in His strength.

Notice in this passage that Paul tells us that we are hard-pressed, not lightly pressed. There does, though, seem to be an odd contradiction when we read Jesus' words from Matthew 11.

> "Come to me, all who labor and are heavy laden, and I will give you rest. Take my yoke upon you, and learn from me, for I am gentle and lowly in heart, and you will find rest for your souls. For my yoke is easy, and my burden is light."
>
> Matthew 11:28-30

We need to keep in mind where this peace comes from that makes His burden so light. It IS NOT contradictory at all but when taken with the whole of Scripture it makes perfect sense.

> Rejoice in the Lord always; again, I will say, rejoice. Let your reasonableness be known to everyone. The Lord is at hand; do not be anxious about anything, but in everything by prayer and supplication with thanksgiving let your requests be made known to God. And the peace of God, which surpasses all understanding, will guard your hearts and your minds in Christ Jesus.
>
> Philippians 4:4-7

It is the peace that Jesus has given me in abundance throughout this journey and His peace that helps when I start to think about my family gathered around a casket as they celebrate the life that He has allowed me to have. That is when it starts to hurt, and I find the need to cry out to Him and fall once again at His feet where I find the peace that I need as I hold on to that lengthening rope.

Perplexed but not in despair

Have you ever uttered the prayer, "Why me, oh God? Why is this happening?" Questions like, "Where was God when my grandson died?" The obvious answer would be, "The same place He was when HIS SON died." I often look around the hospital as I wait for my doctor's appointment or my next radiation treatment and wonder how many of the folks I see waiting are struggling with this disease without Christ. Those who do not have Christ can often be confused over their suffering, often without "hope". It is a horrifying thought to hear a cancer diagnosis, as I well know. Many times, the confusion and despair lead inevitably to a desire to give up, as there is often little hope for those without Christ. I know of a young man who loves music and has all but given up on this because of his lack of hope for a future. We ask, "What did I do wrong? Could I have lived healthier?" But we as disciples are not perplexed or uncertain.

I (we) fully understand one simple thing—it is Christ who is the author of this, and we gratefully submit it to Him and His authority. I have incurable brain cancer because He decided that I would develop incurable brain cancer—it's as simple as that.

> "For I know the plans I have for you, declares the Lord, plans for welfare and not for evil, to give you a future and a hope."
>
> Jeremiah 29:11

> Therefore, preparing your minds for action, and being sober-minded, set your hope fully on the grace that will be brought to you at the revelation of Jesus Christ
>
> 1 Peter 1:3

> And after you have suffered a little while, the God of all grace, who has called you to his eternal glory in Christ, will himself restore, confirm, strengthen, and establish you.
>
> 1 Peter 5:10

> having the eyes of your hearts enlightened, that you may know what is the hope to which he has called you, what are the riches of his glorious inheritance in the saints.
>
> Ephesians 1:18

Sometimes God says "No" to our prayers for healing

Jesus, in answer to prayer, understood that sometimes the Father says, "No" to our most earnest prayers as He did with Jesus' passionate request that the "cup be lifted from Him." God had a plan and Jesus was willing for God to institute that plan. He did not "Name it and Claim it" as many do in today's heretical western churches. Jesus became so distraught that His sweat literally turned to blood. And yet He says, "Not my will but Thine be done." God clearly said, "No" to His request, and thank goodness for it, for we would all be doomed if God had relented!

> And he came out and went, as was his custom, to the Mount of Olives, and the disciples followed him. And when he came to the place, he said to them, "Pray that you may not enter into temptation." And he withdrew from them about a stone's throw, and knelt and prayed, saying, "Father, if you are willing, remove this cup from me. Nevertheless, not my will, but yours, be done." And there appeared to him an angel from heaven, strengthening him. And being in agony he prayed more earnestly; and his sweat became like great drops of blood falling to the ground.
>
> Luke 22:39-45

The Christ in my Cancer

Our ONLY Hope is in Jesus Christ and Him alone. Our hope is NOT in the Doctor's skills, the radiation or chemicals we take to reduce or kill cancer, nor is it in the diet changes. Those things are all necessary and helpful, but they are NOT the reason for our hope!

Clearly, suffering is how God has chosen to bring redemption into a suffering world. Jesus, Himself was a man acquainted with great suffering as shown in Scripture.

> He was despised and rejected by men, a man of sorrows and acquainted with grief; and as one from whom men hide their faces he was despised, and we esteemed him not.
>
> Isaiah 53:3

> Like a sheep he was led to the slaughter and like a lamb before its shearer is silent, so he opens not his mouth. In his humiliation justice was denied him. Who can describe his generation? For his life is taken away from the earth. And the eunuch said to Philip, About whom, I ask you, does the prophet say this, about himself or about someone else? Then Philip opened his mouth, and beginning with this Scripture, he told him the good news about Jesus.
>
> Acts 8:32-35

Jesus, Himself tells us in the book of Luke that He was numbered with the "transgressors" (all those who suffer).

> For I tell you that this Scripture must be fulfilled in me: And he was numbered with the transgressors.
>
> Luke 22:37

If you take just a few minutes to take a look at world events going on around us each day, you will find clear evidence that the world

Suffering and the Disciple of Christ

is full of suffering. Personal suffering and great social suffering are rife within our society. Our societal structure has so broken down that we now see widespread chaos daily within our society—our police are being killed at record rates, our borders are wide-open and fentanyl is killing our children while the leaders that God has placed over us have become corrupt and bereft of any wisdom. (Scripture uses the word fools). So, yes, emotional and spiritual pain has been and always will be an intrinsic part of the human experience. The archetypal example of our suffering was Jesus Christ, who was persecuted and crucified by Roman officials. Suffering will indeed come, but God can give us grace and power to overcome every trial and fulfill our purpose and mission in His kingdom. The Bible gives counsel on the meaning of suffering and how we can best endure it as the following list of scriptures mentioning suffering demonstrate.

Ephesians tells us that in putting on the Armor of God we are told to stand firm. 1 Peter 3 tells us that if we should suffer for what is right, which should be obvious, given if we are putting on the armor correctly (see Part-2 of this book for the armor) and in 'standing' we are truly blessed!

> But even if you should suffer for what is right, you are blessed. Do not fear their threats; do not be frightened.
>
> 1 Peter 3:14

In his letter to the Galatians, Paul sums up best the attitude we should all have regarding pain, death, and suffering. 1 Peter 4:1 tells us as well that we should arm ourselves to endure suffering just as Christ endured suffering on our behalf.

> I have been crucified with Christ. It is no longer I who live, but Christ who lives in me. And the life I now live in the flesh I live by faith in the Son of God, who loved me and gave himself for me.

The Christ in my Cancer

Galatians 2:20

Therefore, since Christ suffered in his body, arm yourselves also with the same attitude, because whoever suffers in the body is done with sin.

1 Peter 4:1

Suffering a little while and Kingdom priorities

We are all the same. We spend an enormous amount of time and energy pursuing the things that this world and this life have to offer, and we place great value on them. Houses, careers, cars, financial stability, etc. (In truth we fill our lives with the stuff that helps temporarily fill the void that God intended to be filled by Him). The list goes on forever and it is unique to each of us.

The real problem is that we neglect the Heavenly realm for the sake of the earthly realm. For those of us who have heard words such as 'Terminal' and 'incurable,' it tends to—or certainly should at least—remove our priorities from the earthly kingdom and laser focus them on the heavenly Kingdom. And as Christ Himself prayed, we should always remember that it is not to be 'Our Will' that is accomplished but 'God's Will that is done,' recognizing that it is in Christ Jesus that God will provide what is needed for us to remain Strong, Firm, and Steadfast as He pours His spirit over us.

> Come now, you who say, Today or tomorrow we will go into such and such a town and spend a year there and trade and make a profit—yet you do not know what tomorrow will bring. What is your life? For you are a mist that appears for a little time and then vanishes. Instead, you ought to say, If the Lord wills, we will live and do this or that.
>
> James 4:13-15

Suffering and the Disciple of Christ

> And the God of all grace, who called you to his eternal glory in Christ, after you have suffered a little while, will himself restore you and make you strong, firm, and steadfast.
>
> 1 Peter 5:10

The man from George Street (Frank Jenner)

A little white-haired man who made a huge impact for the Gospel.

This all started several years ago in a Baptist church in Crystal Palace in South London. The Sunday morning service was closing, and a man stood up at the back and raised his hand, and said: "Excuse me pastor can I share a short testimony?" The pastor looked at his watch and said, "You have two minutes." The man proceeded with his story: "I've just moved into this area. I used to live in Sydney Australia. Just a few months back I was visiting some relatives and I was walking down George Street. You know where George Street is in Sydney going from the Business Area out to the colonial area. A strange little white-haired man stepped out from a shop doorway, put a pamphlet in my hand, and said: 'Excuse me, sir, are you saved, if you die tonight are you going to heaven?' I was astounded by these words. No one had ever asked me that. I thanked him courteously and all the way home to London this puzzled me. I called a friend and thank God he was a Christian and he led me to Christ."

The Baptists love testimonies like that. Everyone applauded and welcomed him into their fellowship. The Baptist pastor flew to Adelaide, Australia the next week, and 10 days later in the middle of a three-day series in a Baptist church in Adelaide, a woman came up to him for some counseling. He wanted to establish where she stood with Christ. She said, "I used to live in Sydney and just a couple of months back I was visiting some friends in Sydney and doing some last-minute shopping down George Street. A strange little white-haired man stepped out of a shop doorway and offered me a pamphlet and said, 'Excuse me, madam, are you saved, if you die tonight are you going to heaven?" I was disturbed by those words. When I got home to Adelaide, I knew this Baptist church was on the next block from me. I sought out the pastor and he led me to Christ. So, I am telling you that I am a Christian.

The London pastor was now very puzzled. Twice in two weeks, he had heard the same testimony. He then flew to preach in the Mount Pleasant Church in Perth. When his teaching series was over the senior elder of that Church took him out for a meal and he asked the elder how he got saved. "I grew up in this church from the age of 15. I never made a commitment to Jesus, just hopped on the bandwagon like everyone else. Because of my business ability, I grew into a place of influence. I was on a business trip to Sydney just three years ago. An obnoxious spiteful little man stepped out of a shop doorway, offered me a religious pamphlet, and accosted me with a question: 'Excuse me, sir, are you saved, if you die tonight are you going to heaven?' I tried to tell him I was a Baptist elder. He wouldn't listen to me. I was seething with anger all the way home from Sydney to Perth. I told my pastor, thinking that he would sympathize, but he agreed. He had been disturbed for years knowing that I didn't have a relationship with Jesus, and he was right. My pastor led me to Jesus just three years ago."

The London preacher flew home and was soon speaking at the Keswick conventions in the Lake District, and he threw in these three testimonies. At the close of this teaching series, four elderly pastors came up and explained that they too had been saved between 25 and 30 years earlier through that same little man on George Street, offering them a pamphlet and asking that same question.

The following week he flew to a similar Keswick convention in the Caribbean for missionaries. He shared the same testimonies. At the close of his teaching, three missionaries came forward and said that they had also been saved between 15 and 25 years earlier by that same little man's testimony and the same question on George Street in Sydney.

Next, he stopped in Atlanta, Georgia to speak at a Naval Chaplain convention. Here for three days, he spoke to over 1000 Naval Chaplains. Afterward, the Chaplain General took him out for a meal, and he asked the Chaplain how he became a Christian. "It was miraculous.

Suffering and the Disciple of Christ

I was a rating on a Naval battleship, and I lived a reprobate life. We were doing exercises in the South Pacific, and we docked at Sydney harbor for replenishments. We hit King's Cross with a vengeance. I was blind drunk, got on the wrong bus, and got off on George Street. As I got off the bus, I thought I saw a ghost as this man jumped out in front of me, pushed a pamphlet in my hand, and said, Sailor, are you saved, if you die tonight are you going to heaven? The fear of God hit me immediately. I was shocked sober, ran back to the ship, and sought out the Chaplain. He led me to Christ. I soon began to prepare for the ministry under his guidance. I am now in charge of 1000 chaplains who are bent on soul-winning today."

Six months later that London pastor flew to a conference for 5,000 Indian missionaries in a remote part of NE India. In the end, the head missionary took him to his humble little home for a simple meal. He asked how he as a Hindu came to Christ.

"I grew up in a very privileged position; I worked in the Indian Diplomatic Mission, and I traveled the world. I am so glad for the forgiveness of Christ and the blood covering my sin. I would be very embarrassed if people found out what I got into. One period of diplomatic service took me to Sydney. I was doing some last-minute shopping, laden with toys and clothes for my children. I was walking down George Street when a courteous white-haired little man stepped out in front of me and offered me a pamphlet and said, 'Excuse me, sir, are you saved, if you die tonight are you going to heaven?' I thanked him very much, but this disturbed me. I got back to my town and sought out our Hindu priest. He couldn't help me, but he advised me that to satisfy my curious mind, I should go and talk to the missionary in the mission home at the end of the road. That was good advice because that day the missionary led me to Christ. I quit Hinduism immediately and began to prepare for ministry. I left the Diplomatic Service and here I am today, by God's grace in charge of all these missionaries who have together led 100,000 people to Christ."

Eight months later the London Pastor was preaching in Sydney. He asked the local Baptist Minister if he knew of a little elderly white-haired man who handed out tracts on George Street. He replied, "Yes I do, his name is Mr. Jenner, although I don't think he does it anymore because he is so frail and elderly."

Two nights later they went to meet him in his little apartment. They knocked on the door and this tiny frail old man greeted them. He sat them down and made them tea. He was so frail that he was slopping the tea into the saucer as his hands shook. The London preacher sat there and told him of all these accounts from the previous three years. This little man sat with tears running down his cheeks. He told them his story.

"I was an enlisted man on an Australian warship. I was living a shameless life. In a crisis, I really hit the wall. One of my colleagues, to whom I gave literal hell, was there to help me. He led me to Jesus and the change in my life was night today in 24 hours. I was so grateful to God; I promised God that I would share Jesus in a simple witness with at least 10 people a day. As God gave me strength, I did that. Sometimes I was ill and couldn't do it, but I made up for the days I missed at other times. I wasn't paranoid about it. I have done this for over 40 years. In my retirement years, the best place was on St. George Street where I saw hundreds of people a day. I got lots of rejections, but a lot of people courteously took the tract. In 40 years of doing this, I have never heard of one single person coming to Jesus until today."

You know, I would say that he must be committed to showing gratitude and love for Jesus to do that for 40 years and not hear of any results. That simple little non-charismatic Baptist man witnessed to perhaps 147,000 people. I think that God was showing that a Baptist pastor from London was the tip of the iceberg. Goodness knows how many more had been arrested for Christ, doing huge jobs out in the mission fields.

Mr. Jenner died two weeks later. Can you imagine the reward when he went home to be in Heaven? I doubt his face would ever have appeared in Charisma Magazine. I doubt there would ever have been a photograph and a write-up in Billy Graham's Decision magazine. No one except a little group of Baptists in Sydney knew about Mr. Jenner, but I tell you his name was famous in Heaven.

Suffering and the Disciple of Christ

Heaven knew Mr. Jenner and you can imagine the welcome and red carpet and the fanfare that he received when he went home to Glory. The End.

Frank Jenner, in his own way, and to the embarrassment of some Christians, got to the heart of the issue: He directly challenged sailors about their standing before God. His simple question is not a formula for us to copy, but his life is a wonderful testimony of how God can use those who remain faithful to him.

> The harvest truly is plentiful, but the laborers are few. Therefore, pray the Lord of the harvest to send out laborers into His harvest.
>
> Matthew 9:37-38

> For our light and momentary troubles are achieving for us an eternal glory that far outweighs them all
>
> 2 Corinthians 4:17.

> In bringing many sons and daughters to glory, it was fitting that God, for whom and through whom everything exists, should make the pioneer of their salvation perfect through what he suffered.
>
> Hebrews 2:10

> In fact, everyone who wants to live a godly life in Christ Jesus will be persecuted.
>
> 2 Timothy 3:12

> Now I rejoice in what I am suffering for you, and I fill up in my flesh what is still lacking in regard to Christ's afflictions, for the sake of his body, which is the church.
>
> Colossians 1:24

Our assurance is in Christ through anything we may endure. He has promised to never 'leave us or forsake us

The Christ in my Cancer

> When you pass through the waters, I will be with you; and when you pass through the rivers, they will not sweep over you. When you walk through the fire, you will not be burned; the flames will not set you ablaze.
>
> Isaiah 43:2

If Christ was despised and rejected by mankind, then those who are His can expect the very same for us. We really need to stop this "Name it and Claim it" nonsense.

> He was despised and rejected by mankind, a man of suffering, and familiar with pain. Like one from whom people hide their faces he was despised, and we held him in low esteem.
>
> Isaiah 53:3

> Blessed is the one who perseveres under trial because, having stood the test, that person will receive the crown of life that the Lord has promised to those who love him.
>
> James 1:12

Jesus tells us in the book of John, that His desire is for us to be at Peace throughout our trials and sufferings, but also tells us to "Take Heart" for He has overcome the world!

> I have told you these things, so that in me you may have peace. In this world you will have trouble. But take heart! I have overcome the world.
>
> John 16:33

It can be tough watching folks sit in the radiation waiting room with looks of despair and tribulation. I truly don't know how anyone could go deal with a cancer diagnosis and not have the God of creation to lean heavily against! But they are many. If we do not repent of our

Suffering and the Disciple of Christ

sins and turn to Christ for our hope and our salvation then we are truly lost as we cannot be a disciple of Christ.

> And whoever does not carry their cross and follow me cannot be my disciple.
>
> Luke 14:7

I am apparently thick sometimes when it comes to learning what God has in mind for me and in that, I can say with the Psalmist that it was good for me to be afflicted, because it realigned my priorities significantly as I learned what He has decreed for me. As I have said earlier in this book, this is Christ's testimony, and it was written for me before creation began.

> It was good for me to be afflicted so that I might learn your decrees.
>
> Psalm 119:72

> I consider that our present sufferings are not worth comparing with the glory that will be revealed in us.
>
> Romans 8:18

> Who shall separate us from the love of Christ? Shall trouble or hardship or persecution or famine or nakedness or danger or sword?
>
> Romans 8:35

> Praise be to the God and Father of our Lord Jesus Christ, the Father of compassion and the God of all comfort, who comforts us in all our troubles, so that we can comfort those in any trouble with the comfort we ourselves receive from God.
>
> 2 Corinthians 1:3-4

> Beloved, do not be surprised at the fiery trial when it comes upon you to test you, as though something strange were happening to you. But rejoice insofar as you share Christ's sufferings, that you may also rejoice and be glad when his glory is revealed.
>
> 1 Peter 4: 12-13

Pure Joy—We are to face the trials and suffering in our lives with the joy that only God can provide

> Consider it pure joy, my brothers, and sisters, whenever you face trials of many kinds, because you know that the testing of your faith produces perseverance. Let perseverance finish its work so that you may be mature and complete, not lacking anything.
>
> James 1:2-4

> Not only so, but we also glory in our sufferings, because we know that suffering produces perseverance; perseverance, character; and character, hope. And hope does not put us to shame, because God's love has been poured out into our hearts through the Holy Spirit, who has been given to us.
>
> Romans 5:3-5

CHAPTER 2

Peace Amidst the Storm

The First Bucket List trip is "In the Books" in Colonial Williamsburg. My wife and I just spent time together while we still can. Spent 5 days in one of the old "Colonial Rooms"—super cool. I really do enjoy the old architecture and history. Ate entirely too much and slept a lot (which was good—radiation recovery). Due to the back pain from my seizure, I had to stop every few yards to sit on a bench, but at least they were regularly spaced. And the straw mattress could have been more comfortable. Oh—and . . . so far my wife hasn't killed me with her driving. Seriously she is fantastic and doing a great job—I am the one who can't sit in the passenger seat without losing my mind.

We are now on Facebook at Mikaal Cooper, on YouTube at GreyMattersMinisteries, and on Telegram at GreyMattersMinistries and if you go to Rumble.com and search for channels under Grey_Matters—The Restoration of Intellect. Please subscribe to any of these if you get the opportunity.

Scott

So how can we know there is peace in the firestorm? This "Peace amidst the Storm" is not a 'feeling," but is instead an understanding based on knowledge and experience.

The Christ in my Cancer

In Question 33, the Westminster Shorter Catechism[1] defines Justification as "An act of God's free grace, wherein he pardons all of our sins, and accepts us a righteous in his sight, only for the righteousness of Christ imputed to us and received by Faith Alone."

> Webster's Dictionary defines Justification as "the act of justifying something—vindication through arguments offered".[2]

Justification by Faith Alone. It is one of the primary tenets of the reformed Christian faith . . . .

But what exactly does that mean?

Faith has 3 basic parts to it . . . Faith is Intellectual, Faith is Experiential, Faith is Fiduciary.

Faith is Knowing Christ, Loving Christ, and Trusting Christ in a way that is both active and growing. It is not leaping blindly in the dark or believing for no reason at all. It is not self-reliant, perfect, or stagnant but always leads to obedience and the bearing of much fruit. It begins small and grows throughout a believer's lifetime.

What does it mean to be Justified? It means to be found righteous in God's eyes?

To be declared virtuous and blameless concluding the full presentation of evidence.

> Webster's Dictionary defines Righteousness as "morally right or justifiable; virtuous".[2]

---

1 The Westminster Shorter Catechism - The Presbytery of the United States: The Free Church of Scotland (continuing). https://www.westminsterconfession.org/resources/confessional-standards/the-westminster-shorter-catechism/ Viewed October 11, 2022

2 Webster's Dictionary: https://www.merriam-webster.com/dictionary/ Viewed October 11, 2022

One who is Righteous has met or exceeded every single requirement that God has outlined in His Word and following the presentation of all evidence is found to be blameless and pure. A righteous one can be justified. An unrighteous one cannot possibly be justified.

To be Justified (declared virtuous and blameless) means that the Omniscient (all-knowing) has examined your every motive, thought, and deed and found them to be Righteous (pure, morally right) according to His standards (not ours). So, to be Justified means to have a just or right reputation in God's eyes which means never having disobeyed even a single one of His commands, leading a wholly upright, righteous, and God-glorifying life from birth to death.

The Covenant of Works

Are we or have we ever been justified in God's eyes? Ask many people, "If you died right now and stood before God would you be found guilty or innocent?" Inevitably the answer is always "Innocent for a variety of reasons . . ."

I have never cheated on my wife, or I never killed anybody. All of these pertain to our own standards of guilt or innocence but fall far short of God's Holy standards.

Genesis chapters 1 and 2 tell us, in part, the story of man's creation and subsequent fall . . .

At the end of Chapter 1, we see that God has created man in His own image and declares that, "it was very good". When God declares that, "it was very good," it was not just His opinion, but it was a Judicial Declaration! This same Synonymous Parallelism (the Hebraic habit of stating the same truth two different ways) is also used elsewhere in Scripture.

> So, you will walk in the way of the good and keep to the paths of the righteous
>
> Proverbs 2:20

We see from the text then when God declares that man was "very good," He is declaring him as righteous. Remember that this is just after God created them and before their disobedience at the tree. We must also remember though that while God credits Adam and Eve with righteousness, it was still unproven and unearned righteousness. They were only righteous at that point because they had not sinned yet!

In the final passage of Genesis 1, we also see a covenant declared by God between Himself and His new creation in which Adam had two primary responsibilities.

First, Adam was to refrain from eating from the tree of knowledge.—The test of obedience so as to "prove his righteousness." If he was faithful and obedient to the commands of God his faith would no longer be untested and unproven. Second, he was to "be fruitful and multiply," thus increasing God's image across this new planet and bringing Him eternal glory!

This first covenant between God and man was a covenant of Works. Mankind had to earn his righteousness through strict obedience to God. Sadly, we know what happened... Adam disobeyed God and became subject to the punishment God had warned him about—death.

But God, instead of punishing them as He had promised, was merciful in that He did not immediately cast them into Hell. They were cast out of the Garden, they suffered both spiritual and physical death, they were both now wholly incapable of offering God the obedience He required and were therefore doomed to live separated from the benevolent presence of the Lord!

But God also gave them a promise of great hope—One which would count to them as righteousness...

> I will put enmity between you and the woman, and between your offspring and her offspring; he shall bruise your head, and you shall bruise his heel.
>
> Genesis 3:15

The Covenant of Grace

Contrary to the First Covenant between God and man in which righteousness was earned by works, this Covenant between God and man was one of Unmerited Grace.

The Westminster Catechism puts it this way: "Man, by his fall, having made himself incapable of life by that covenant, [1] the Lord was pleased to make a second, commonly called the Covenant of Grace, whereby He freely offers unto sinners life and salvation by Jesus Christ, requiring of them faith in Him, that all may be saved; and promising to give unto all those who are ordained unto eternal life His Holy Spirit, to make them willing and able to believe."[3]

> Webster's Dictionary defines imputation as "to credit or ascribe (something) to a person or a cause."[4]

And Adam took shelter in the Covenant of God's Grace as evidenced in the fact that he gave his wife a new name—no longer would she be called wife, but Eve . . .

Adam named his wife Eve because she would become the mother of all the living. The name Eve literally means Giver of Life.

Genesis 3:20

Adam's faith was not introspective, looking back at his error and pining to repair the damage he had done through "better living," but instead he now looked to "the seed of the woman" to cover his

---

3 Sproul, R.C., *The Promises of God: Discovering the One Who Keeps His Word*: David C Cook. 2013 pg. 108
4 Webster's Dictionary: https://www.merriam-webster.com/dictionary/ Viewed October 11, 2022

nakedness. Through this "seed" Adam knew that they would be restored to God and would once again dwell forever in His presence!

This is emblematic of their spiritual nakedness as well. They stood before God, covering themselves in fig leaves as He tells them that one day, He would forever cover their nakedness and clothe them in the righteous robes of His only Son!

A Hard Reboot—Noah and the Flood

As we move further into the Genesis story we find that following these events, mankind, true to his now fallen nature, quickly degenerates yet again into endless sin and rebellion against God.

> The Lord saw that the wickedness of man was great in the earth, and that every intention of the thoughts of his heart was only evil continually.
>
> Genesis 6:5

This continues to this very day!

As a result of this rampantly corruptible behavior, God decided to judge creation and start again with the only man that "found favor in the eyes of the Lord"—Noah. We all know the story.

God would return the Earth to its pre-sin state of Genesis 1:2 through the flood.

> How the earth was corrupt in God's sight, and the earth was filled with violence. And God saw the earth, and behold, it was corrupt, for all flesh had corrupted their way on the earth. And God said to Noah, I have determined to make an end of all flesh, for the earth is filled with violence through them. Behold, I will destroy them with the earth.
>
> Genesis 6:11-13

We all know how that went don't we? Noah did about as well as his ancestors in the "not sinning against God" department. In an eerie reminder of the Garden fall, Noah sinned in a garden vineyard by consuming too much of the fruit of the vine and became drunk, and was found lying naked before God.

> Noah began to be a man of the soil, and he planted a vineyard. He drank of the wine and became drunk and lay uncovered in his tent.
>
> Genesis 9:20-21

A shift in methodology

The account of Noah's fall, just as with Adam, ended in both curse and blessing.

> Now the Lord said to Abram, Go from your country and your kindred and your father's house to the land that I will show you. And I will make of you a great nation, and I will bless you and make your name great, so that you will be a blessing. I will bless those who bless you, and him who dishonors you I will curse, and in you all the families of the earth shall be blessed.
>
> Genesis 12:1-3

This is a remarkable statement—No longer will God ask his servants to "be fruitful and multiply," as was the case with Adam and Noah, but God would take the reins Himself and HE would now multiply His church in all the Earth.

What Adam and Noah failed to do God would now do Himself through His promise to Abraham.

It is important to understand that God's promise to Abraham is a continuation of His promise to Adam and Eve that the "seed of the woman" would conquer the "seed of the serpent".

Continuing forward through the Genesis account we come to one of the most critical passages in Scripture when it comes to the doctrine of Sola Fide (Faith Alone). God made Abraham a promise that He would make a great nation of his descendants, and that through his bloodline, God would bless all of the families of the Earth. Now we all know Abraham had some bumps along the way to the fulfillment of this promise by God, but aside from the fact that Noah was flawed and fallen, he BELIEVED God and it was this faith that was counted to him as righteousness!

> And behold, the word of the Lord came to him . . . your very own son shall be your heir. And he brought him outside and said, Look toward heaven, and number the stars, if you are able to number them. Then he said to him, So shall your offspring be. And he believed the Lord, and he counted it to him as righteousness.
>
> Genesis 15:4-6

Looking at the sentence "And he (Abraham) believed the Lord, and he (God) counted it to him as righteousness." we think of the word imputation.

When Scripture tells us that God "counts" Abraham's belief as righteousness, it means that God is imputing His own righteousness to Abraham because of his belief. It was for Abraham's belief in God's promise alone that God declared him as righteous—certainly not for his obedience as Scripture clearly shows. Abraham certainly did believe God or God would not have declared him righteous, but Abraham sinned in that he did not wait on God to fulfill His promise but took the fulfillment of it into his own hands instead.

> So, after Abram had lived ten years in the land of Canaan, Sarai, Abram's wife, took Hagar the Egyptian, her servant, and gave her to Abram her husband as a wife.
>
> Genesis 16:3

Scripture itself further clarifies the matter for us in eliminating justification by any means other than by Sola Gratia (Grace Alone.)

> What then shall we say was gained by Abraham, our forefather according to the flesh? For if Abraham was justified by works, he has something to boast about, but not before God. For what does the Scripture say? Abraham believed God, and it was counted to him as righteousness. Now to the one who works, his wages are not counted as a gift but as his due. And to the one who does not work but believes in him who justifies the ungodly, his faith is counted as righteousness.
>
> Romans 4:1-5

Fulfillment

Genealogically proven—The Old Testament is rife with family trees and genealogies, and while many of us just skim over these, they are important. These long passages of "begats" detail for us the lineage of 'the seed of the woman' from Abraham to Christ.

As the Son of God emerged from the waters of baptism, the Holy Spirit of God descended upon Him and lead Him into the wilderness to be tempted for 40 days and remained obedient to the Father throughout it all.

In all things and at all times, Jesus Christ was obedient.

> Have this mind among yourselves, which is yours in Christ Jesus, who, though he was in the form of God, did not count equality with God a thing to be grasped, but emptied himself, by taking the form of a servant, being born in the likeness of men. And being found in human form, he humbled himself by becoming obedient to the point of death, even death on a cross. Therefore God has highly exalted him and bestowed on him the name that is above every name, so that at the name of Jesus every knee should bow, in heaven and on earth and under the earth, and every tongue confess that Jesus Christ is Lord, to the glory of God the Father.
>
> Philippians 2:5-11

There is another differentiation in this passage that harkens back to Genesis.

Mankind fell because Adam, through the serpent's enticing words and the influence of his wife, desired to be like God. This Son of God, this "Second Adam" did not count equality with God as a thing to be grasped, but rather humbled and emptied himself before God.

Jesus Christ is the "seed of the woman" first promised in the Garden—the one through whom God would increase Abraham's seed,' the one who would offer the obedience and righteousness that God required of man.

> Therefore, just as sin came into the world through one man, and death through sin, and so death spread to all men because all sinned ... For if, because of one man's trespass, death reigned through that one man, much more will those who receive the abundance of grace and the free gift of righteousness reign in life through the one-man Jesus Christ. Therefore, as one trespass led to condemnation for all men, so one act of righteousness leads to justification and life for all men. For as by the one man's disobedience the many were made sinners, so by the one man's obedience the many will be made righteous. Now the law came in to increase the trespass, but where sin increased, grace abounded all the more, so that, as sin reigned in death, grace also might reign through righteousness leading to eternal life through Jesus Christ our Lord.
>
> Romans 5:12, 17-21

Penalty Paid

Christ offered unto his heavenly Father the perfect obedience that no one else had been able to offer. Adam had failed in the Garden, Noah failed in the vineyard, and Abraham failed in his tent.

But that only gets to one of the two root problems brought about by the tree.

Christ satisfied God's demand for perfect obedience and righteousness.

Jesus Christ would indeed be welcome into the Kingdom of Heaven—justified by His obedience!

But where at this point does that leave us? We are still under the condemnation that hangs over us from the fall. God cannot simply forgive us; justice must be served.

It was not enough that Jesus Christ lived a perfectly obedient and sinless life because if it simply stopped there, Christ would be the only one God can see as righteous—the rest of us are still irreversibly condemned at this point.

The penalty for our disobedience MUST also be paid. God's Justice MUST be satisfied.

> Righteousness and justice are the foundation of your throne.
>
> Psalm 89:14a

And it is not only our own individual sin that hangs over our heads. Even if we could live a sinless and obedient life (which we can't), we would still be found guilty. It is the imputed sin of Adam that still condemns us!

> Therefore, just as sin came into the world through one man, and death through sin, and so death spread to all men because all sinned.
>
> Romans 5:12

> For all have sinned and fall short of the Glory of God.
>
> Romans 3:23

Jesus Christ would have to do more than simply lead a righteous life Himself. He would need to "step in" and not only lead a perfect life, but He would also need to suffer the penalty for ALL of our sins as well.

> Christ redeemed us from the curse of the law by becoming a curse for us—for it is written, Cursed is everyone who is hanged on a tree—so that in Christ Jesus the blessing of Abraham might come to the Gentiles, so that we might receive the promised Spirit through faith.
>
> Galatians 3:13-14

So that the Blessing of Abraham might also come to the Gentiles… As we saw from Genesis—The "Seed of the Woman" and the "Blessing to Abraham" were not about numbers of descendants, but about Christ's final Victory over the Serpent—the restoration of God's Relationship with Mankind through His Sacrifice on our behalf!

Jesus Christ "drank the cup of the wrath of God" on our behalf so that we would not have to. Christ took 100% of the wrath of the Father upon Himself for all those who would put true faith in Him and look to Him for their Salvation! God chose to IMPUTE our sins and disobedience upon His Son on that cross at Calvary and at the same time He imputed Christ's righteousness upon us so that He now sees any who believe (True Faith) as having the righteousness of Jesus Christ! Through the means of His life, God's imputation, and His Sacrifice, Jesus Christ has taken the wrath of Almighty God on behalf of His Church!

And yet, that doesn't really complete everything, does it? As we saw in the beginning, justification is about "Proof." To be justified as righteous means that the burden of proof has been established to the satisfaction of the court. While many Christians focus on the life and death of Christ as the central tenets of our faith, many miss the most integral component of the Gospel Message—the Resurrection of Jesus Christ from the Dead!

Peace Amidst the Storm

The Resurrection piece of the story is key because if death was able to hold Christ then His crucifixion would have been legitimate as this would have proven him an imposter. It was only in the resurrection that He removed any doubt that He was indeed exactly who He said He was!

The Resurrection piece of the story tells us that the power of sin and death has indeed been broken and that in Christ we are truly set free from the death that has hung over our heads since Eden. And most importantly the Resurrection piece of the story tells us that God has indeed accepted Christ's sacrifice for mankind's sins and that Jesus Christ to this day sits at the right hand of God the Father. continuously interceding on our behalf.

We find in the resurrection the strongest possible assurance of pardon and peace. When Christ rose on Easter morning, He left behind Him in the depths of the grave every one of our sins; there they remain buried from the sight of God so completely that they will not be able to rise up against us anymore.

Adam disobeyed God when he sought to be "like" God and ate of the tree from which he was forbidden. As a result, Adam's sin has been imputed to his descendants such that ALL have sinned and fallen short of the Glory of God. Yet God, in His mercy, withheld judgment and offered a promise . . . a promise that one day, God would provide a way that would restore the relationship that had been lost through Adam's disobedience, a "seed" that would bring about final victory against the serpent. A blessing was given to Abraham as a reward for his faith.

Millenia of mankind's activity upon this Earth has proven that when Scripture speaks of the Total Depravity of Mankind, it knows from whence it speaks. From Cain and Able to the present day, man's inhumanity to man still rages on.

Man, left to his own devices CANNOT possibly provide for his own redemption. He can never be justified as righteous before God without the direct intervention of God Himself!

Jesus Christ, through His perfect obedience, atoning sacrifice, and resurrection from the dead is the only possible way where those who have a true and living faith (a gift from God, by the way) can be declared by God (Justified) to be Righteous in His sight and thus be saved.

Justification is a legal declaration whereby God judges the one who looks to Christ by Faith to be Righteous in His sight. We must be Justified by faith alone and not our works. One of the consequences of the indwelling presence of sin is that we are wholly incapable of offering God the obedience He requires.

A True and Living Faith is not introspective—looking within to see what we can do to save ourselves. Rather it is extra perspective—looking outside of ourselves to what Christ has done.

True Faith begins with Him—A Gift from God to His chosen so that no one can boast. Faith offers nothing, accomplishes nothing, brings nothing, and earns nothing. Faith is at best a diseased, crippled, and palsied hand that is capable of doing nothing except receiving that which God freely gives!

True Faith is not a blind leap or some mystical belief in the unbelievable. Faith is an intellectual understanding of God through His Word—who He is and what His divine will is.

Faith is Knowledge

First and Foremost, knowledge is revealed through His Spirit as we continue in the study of His Word. But we can also gain knowledge through the study of history itself, the study of languages and cultures from when the Scriptures were written, and the study of historians from the day and their remaining records.

Knowledge is rooted in Doctrine

Doctrine roots us in the truth of God's Word. Knowledge of His Word keeps us from straying onto "the path that leads to destruction." Without proper doctrine, we will ultimately fall prey to the philosophy of the society in which we live. Proper doctrine is commanded by God.

The proper doctrine protects us from error. For Jesus, the proper doctrine was certainly not irrelevant. It was the primary means by which men and women will become His followers! Rutherford and

Calvin would often speak of the concepts of Faith without Doctrine and Pious Ignorance.

True Faith is found in Relationship

Scripture shows us that the relationship we have with Christ is THE most intimate relationship we will ever experience!

A true and saving faith not only has an intellectual understanding of God through His word, but it also has an intimate, ongoing growing relationship with Jesus Christ—loving Him and clinging to Him with all our heart!

True Faith is found in Trust

Christians are to trust in Christ and Christ Alone—not in themselves, not in their own abilities or resources, not in the government or any other person, not even in the Church, the Pastor, the Sunday School Teacher, etc.! Our trust is built on knowledge gained through experience and inspection. Simply put—we cannot trust God unless we have first experienced God! Christian faith trusts Christ, not because it is a blind leap but precisely because it knows Him!

Faith can be exceedingly small indeed and still be a genuine Faith. **It is not about the quantity or quality of our faith that matters but it is about the reality of our faith.**

It's not a strong faith or a mature faith that wins the victory and receives the gift of eternal life, but the weak and small faith that reaches out for Christ with a shriveled and palsied hand just to touch the hem of His garment! Faith is knowing Christ, loving Christ, and Trusting Christ in a way that is both active and growing.

It is not leaping blindly in the dark or believing for no reason at all. It is not self-reliant, perfect, or stagnant but always leads to obedience and the bearing of much fruit. It begins small and grows throughout a believer's lifetime.

Faith Knows; Faith Loves; Faith Trusts; Faith Acts; Faith Grows. It is by THIS Faith that we are Justified in God's sight—Declared Righteous & Adopted as Sons and Daughters of the Most-High King

CHAPTER 3

The Hope and Humility of Jesus Christ

The second Bucket List trip is "In the Books" at Belhurst Castle on the Finger Lakes in New York. We spent the week just sitting on one of the park benches they had there, looking out over the lake and watching things like birds, boats, squirrels, beavers, leaves, wind, trees, boats, and trains. SUPER RELAXING. This was a very necessary trip though as it was wonderfully relaxing.

We found an artisan cheese shop and went for a "cheese tasting" paired with wine. Excellent cheese—still have some we are slowly eating in the fridge. (My son has a sticker on the car he is letting us use that says "Birds Aren't Real". I should kick his backside—it's just plain embarrassing).

Scott

> The book of the genealogy of Jesus Christ, the son of David, the son of Abraham. Abraham was the father of Isaac, and Isaac the father of Jacob, and Jacob the father of Judah and his brothers, and Judah the father of Perez and Zerah by Tamar, and Perez the father of Hezron, and Hezron the father of Ram, and Ram the father of Amminadab, and Amminadab the father of Nahshon, and Nahshon the father of Salmon, and Salmon the father of Boaz by Rahab, and Boaz the father of Obed by

Ruth, and Obed the father of Jesse, and Jesse the father of David the king. And David was the father of Solomon by the wife of Uriah, and Solomon the father of Rehoboam, and Rehoboam the father of Abijah, and Abijah the father of Asaph, and Asaph the father of Jehoshaphat, and Jehoshaphat the father of Joram, and Joram the father of Uzziah, and Uzziah the father of Jotham, and Jotham the father of Ahaz, and Ahaz the father of Hezekiah, and Hezekiah the father of Manasseh, and Manasseh the father of Amos, and Amos the father of Josiah, and Josiah the father of Jechoniah and his brothers, at the time of the deportation to Babylon. And after the deportation to Babylon: Jechoniah was the father of Shealtiel, and Shealtiel the father of Zerubbabel, and Zerubbabel the father of Abiud, and Abiud the father of Eliakim, and Eliakim the father of Azor, and Azor the father of Zadok, and Zadok the father of Achim, and Achim the father of Eliud, and Eliud the father of Eleazar, and Eleazar the father of Matthan, and Matthan the father of Jacob, and Jacob the father of Joseph the husband of Mary, of whom Jesus was born, who is called Christ. So all the generations from Abraham to David were fourteen generations, and from David to the deportation to Babylon fourteen generations, and from the deportation to Babylon to the Christ fourteen generations.

Matthew 1:1-17

The Hope for Mankind

Jesus Christ came to save all mankind from the sin inherent in us all as a result of Adam's original sin in the Garden of Eden. As a result of Adam's sin, a substitute was required. The sacrifice of a second Adam, sinless in every way, born of woman, was necessary for God's judgment of sinful man to be satisfied. Nothing short of this sacrifice of righteousness could accomplish this redemptive action. None can be saved without fully embracing and accepting this redemptive act accomplished on the cross of Calvary, faith in the sinless life of this "God-Man", faith in the satisfaction of God's wrath through His death on the cross, and faith in the resurrection of this Savior. Since "all have sinned", only God Himself could live so perfect a life as to become "sin" for us so that we could become "His righteousness", thus satisfying the "foundational" character of God's justice. However, this "second Adam" must be fully man for the sins of man to be "accounted unto Him". God's own Son, Jesus Christ, accomplished this by entering the "line of men" as described in these opening verses of the gospel of Matthew.

Matthew chapter 1, verse 1, therefore, is a message of both "hope" and humiliation." Hope for mankind—Humiliation for God's own Son!

Chances are, your eyes began to "glaze over" as we read this genealogical record Matthew puts forth in this passage, but we need to remember two things about Scripture as we begin.

Both are found in 2 Timothy 3:16-17.

First—"All Scripture is breathed out by God . . ." And second—"All Scripture is . . . profitable for teaching, for reproof, for correction, and for training in righteousness, that the man of God may be complete, equipped for every good work."

Understanding then these two points, we need to take special note of the placement of this passage in Matthew 1:1-17. This passage immediately opens the first of the 4 Gospels. This passage ALSO opens the entire New Testament Scriptures. It is the very first passage of the very first book of the "New" Testament, so we should infer that God has placed a very high priority on this genealogy.

But Why did God place so much importance on this genealogy? While some folks today are very involved in tracing their family tree, most place very little importance on genealogy. Not so for the Jews, to whom this book was primarily written. Matthew was, after all, a Jew himself. The Jews (even today) are extremely interested in genealogy, for in it they look for the Messiah. The one who will set them free and restore the Jewish people to their rightful place with God.

It was also genealogy that determined which tribes were given land and wealth, and this existed well into Jesus' time. One could not buy or sell land without documented proof that it was theirs to "trade" and must be demonstrated not only by a "bill of sale" but must also be shown that those involved in the transactions had "inherited" rights to the property as "ancestral permission" so to speak.

> Moses commanded the people of Israel, saying, This is the land that you shall inherit by lot, which the Lord has commanded to give to the nine tribes and to the half-tribe.
>
> Numbers 34:13

> These are the inheritances that the people of Israel received in the land of Canaan, which Eleazar the priest and Joshua the son of Nun and the heads of the fathers' houses of the tribes of the people of Israel gave them to inherit. Their inheritance was by lot, just as the Lord had commanded by the hand of Moses for the nine and one-half tribes. For Moses had given an inheritance to the two and one-half tribes beyond the Jordan, but to the Levites he gave no inheritance among them. For the people of Joseph were two tribes, Manasseh and Ephraim. And no portion was given to the Levites in the land, but only cities to dwell in, with their pasturelands for their livestock and their substance. The people of Israel did as the Lord commanded Moses; they allotted the land.
>
> Joshua 14:1-5

This "genealogical record" was also important in the line of the tribe of Levi—the tribe tasked with the "Priesthood" of the entire Jewish people. One could only be chosen as the High Priest once it had been shown that that individual had been given a "divine right" to hold that office as demonstrated by his lineage through the ancestral record.

> The sons of Levi … These are the men whom David put in charge of the service of song in the house of the Lord after the ark rested there. They ministered with song before the tabernacle of the tent of meeting until Solomon built the house of the Lord in Jerusalem, and they performed their service according to their order.
>
> 1 Chronicles 6:1, 31-32

So also, Matthew, right from the outset of his gospel record, set out to prove beyond any doubt, that Jesus Christ was indeed the "Son of Man" and was exactly who He claimed to be.

Notice also that Matthew only traces Jesus' lineage back to Abraham and David instead of all the way back to Adam.

Matthew, being a Jew himself, understood the mindset of the Jewish people, and knew full well that his fellow Jews saw these two men, Abraham and David, as the apex of Jewish religion and as such placed the most significance upon these two men where the Biblical genealogical record was concerned.

> Abraham was the "Father" of the Jewish nation.
> David was the "King" of the Jewish nation.
> The Messiah was to be the "Son of David."

Right from the outset, Matthew was trying to draw a direct line from Abraham, through David, to Jesus Christ as the Messiah, proving to the Jewish people, through the historical record, that Jesus Christ was indeed exactly who He claimed to be. He comes to us through the line of the generations.

The Humility of Christ

> Have this mind among yourselves, which is yours in Christ Jesus, who, though he was in the form of God, did not count equality with God a thing to be grasped, but

emptied himself, by taking the form of a servant, being born in the likeness of men. And being found in human form, he humbled himself by becoming obedient to the point of death, even death on a cross.

Philippians 2:5-8

The genealogy detailed here in Matthew also reveals to us the Godly humility which Christ displayed in emptying Himself of all His "God-ness" and taking on the "flesh" of fallen man!

Jesus Christ left the Glory of God to become like a "fallen man." The Creator became the created.

The Holy became sinful, and The Judge became the judged! The Innocent became the guilty!

Moreover, Jesus did not just inherit a human body that was "pre-fall" perfect, but instead took on a body that was prone to infirmity, decay, sickness, and death.

But humility does not stop with the body alone. He suffered not only a failing physical body, but He also took on the infirmity of a fallen mind and heart, subject to all the same questions, fears, and concerns that we also deal with in our own lives!

A Depraved Genealogy

When we closely examine the genealogy Matthew details in this passage, we also come to understand that Jesus' humility in coming to earth in the form of man was not simply physical and emotional, but also genealogical. We cannot say that "Yes—Jesus may have taken on a physically and emotionally flawed body and heart, but oh, what a proud family tree He comes from," for such is far from the case. Yes, Jesus was indeed descended from Abraham and David, but they were rather corrupt individuals. Abraham was guilty of adultery against his wife Sarah and fathered an illegitimate son by the name of Ishmael.

David was guilty of an adulterous affair and had the husband of his lover killed in battle to justify his actions. Not only does Matthew include women in his genealogical record here, which was not common in his time as all inheritance passed from father to son, but he conspicuously excludes some of the "great" women of God such as Sarah and Hannah, yet he includes women such as Tamar, Rahab, Bathsheba (the wife of Uriah), and Mary, mother of Jesus, each of whose lives tells tragic stories.

> Tamar was King David's daughter and had a brother, Absalom, and a half-brother, Amnon. Amnon had an obsessive desire for his half-sister Tamar, and one day he pretended to be sick and called for her to come to him in his bedroom to help him. When she was there alone with him, he raped her. Although David was angry, he did not punish Amnon or require him to marry Tamar, so Absalom took it upon himself to murder Amnon in revenge. Absalom's anger and bitterness toward his father because of these events eventually led to his attempt to usurp his throne and disgrace David by committing public immorality with his father's concubines.
>
> 2 Samuel 13:1-22
>
> Rahab was a young Canaanite prostitute and as such was not a very likely candidate for a heroine of the faith. Jericho, in which she lived and "worked," was one of the principal seats of idol worship and was especially devoted to Ashtaroth, the goddess of the moon. Here was centered all that was the vilest and most degrading in the religion of the Canaanites.
>
> Joshua 2:1-6
>
> Despite her marital status, David summoned Bathsheba to the palace, and they slept together. Bathsheba later discovered she was pregnant. When the king was told of this, he asked for Uriah to report back to him from the battlefield. David sent him home that evening, hoping

Uriah would sleep with his wife and thus provide a cover for the pregnancy. Instead of obeying orders, Uriah slept in the quarters of the king's servants, refusing to enjoy a respite while his men on the battlefield were still in harm's way, but Uriah did the same thing the next night as well, showing integrity sharp contrast to David's lack thereof. David then commanded his military leader, Joab, to have Uriah placed on the front lines of battle and then to purposefully fall back from him, leaving Uriah exposed to enemy attack. Joab followed the directive, and Uriah was killed in battle. After her time of mourning, Bathsheba married David and gave birth to a son, but the thing David had done displeased the LORD.

2 Samuel 11:2-17

Mary endured the stigma of being pregnant outside of marriage, which was generally considered an act of adultery and therefore a stoning offense for both parties involved.

Matthew 1:18-19

A Gospel proclamation: The opening verses of the Gospel of Matthew detail for us the humbling fact that Jesus Christ took unto Himself a heritage of corruption, prostitution, adultery, and murder.

Jesus, as this genealogy demonstrates, is willing to take unto Himself, the worst that this sinful world has to offer, and if He was willing to humble Himself into this depraved and sinful lineage, is there anything that I have done, or can do that would cause Him to reject me!

We are welcome at His table: This genealogy then is among the most encouraging proclamations of the Gospel message in all of Scripture! If Jesus Christ is not ashamed to take on the depravity of this lineage, how could we ever think that He would be ashamed to take us as well!

The Hope and Humility of Jesus Christ

There are Two Genealogies

A Genealogy of Death.

> And to Adam he said, "Because you have listened to the voice of your wife and have eaten of the tree of which I commanded you, You shall not eat of it, cursed is the ground because of you; in pain you shall eat of it all the days of your life; thorns and thistles it shall bring forth for you; and you shall eat the plants of the field. By the sweat of your face you shall eat bread, till you return to the ground, for out of it you were taken; for you are dust, and to dust you shall return."
>
> Genesis 3:17-19

(And THAT is the unvarnished reason that I have brain cancer!)

> Thus, all the days that Adam lived were 930 years, and he died.
>
> Genesis 5:5
>
> Thus, all the days that Seth lived were 912 years, and he died.
>
> Genesis 5:8
>
> Thus, all the days that Enosh lived were 905 years, and he died.
>
> Genesis 5:11
>
> Thus, all the days that Kenan lived were 910 years, and he died.
>
> Genesis 5:14
>
> Thus, all the days that Enoch lived were 365 years, and he died.
>
> Genesis 5:23

And so on goes the list—Death is the end for all those who are of Adam's genealogy.

A Genealogy of Life

In order then to find the life promised to those who overcome and stay on the narrow road of Matthew 7:13-14, we must be adopted into a new genealogical line.

> Blessed be the God and Father of our Lord Jesus Christ! According to His great mercy, He has caused us to be born again into a living hope through the resurrection of Jesus Christ from the dead!
>
> 1 Peter 1:3

> Therefore, if anyone is in Christ, he is a new creation. The old (genealogy) has passed away, the new (genealogy) has come!
>
> 2 Corinthians 5:17

> "Truly, truly, I say to you, unless one is born of water and the Spirit, he cannot enter the kingdom of God. That which is born of the flesh is flesh, and that which is born of the Spirit is spirit."
>
> John 3:5-6

> In love He predestined us for adoption as sons through Jesus Christ, according to the purpose of his will, to the praise of his glorious grace, with which he has blessed us in the Beloved. In Him we have redemption through his blood, the forgiveness of our trespasses, according to the riches of His grace, which He lavished upon us, in all wisdom and insight making known to us the mystery of His will, according to His purpose, which He set forth in Christ as a plan for the fullness of time, to unite all things in Him, things in heaven and things on earth. In Him we have obtained an inheritance, having been predestined according to the purpose of Him who works all things

according to the counsel of His will, so that we who were the first to hope in Christ might be to the praise of His glory. In Him you also, when you heard the word of truth, the gospel of your salvation, and believed in Him, were sealed with the promised Holy Spirit, who is the guarantee of our inheritance until we acquire possession of it, to the praise of his glory.

Ephesians 1:5-11

So which will it be? Which genealogy will you choose? Will you decide to remain in the genealogy of Adam's death, or choose the genealogy of life in Christ Jesus? Are you too proud to humble yourself before Christ and accept His offer of adoption into His family Tree?

Is He still too good, too high and mighty to be unapproachable? Are your sins still so great that even Christ could not want you to partake of His grace? Will you continue to dwell in the lineage of death as outlined in Genesis chapter 5 or are you ready to accept Christ's offer of redemption and become a new creature through the lineage of Matthew Chapter 1? What life should look like for those who are walking along the hard road of the redemption of Christ Jesus? He is the ONLY exit off of the wide road!

Jesus Christ is NOT ASHAMED to call us sons and daughters! He is NOT too proud to offer His life for the worst of us. He humbled Himself and took on our corrupt flesh so that he could call murderers, adulterers, liars, and thieves members of His family, His heirs, His brothers, and His sisters!

It is at the cross of Calvary where this transaction takes place. It is at the cross where we can exchange our lineage of corruption and death for the lineage of life and forgiveness that only God can provide! It is at His table that we can sit with the God of the universe and partake of the life that is waiting at the end of the hard road!

It is at the Lord's table where the Creator of ALL THINGS awaits to call the very worst of sinners FAMILY and to wash their feet of the filth of this world and offer to them the purity of His righteousness!

It is at the cross where this lowly, meek King of the universe poured out His blood and offered His body as the only sacrifice worthy of satisfying God's judgment for sin, and it is at His table where we are invited to sit with Him and partake of His rest, His peace, His reward in Heaven!

As we drink of His cup and eat the bread of His salvation tonight, let us all remember the genealogy of sin which He so willingly took upon Himself, so that we in turn could be covered with the righteousness of the only begotten Son of God, the One in whom the Father is "well pleased."

CHAPTER 4

The Wide and Narrow Gates

Colonial Williamsburg: While Scott spent time resting, I had the chance to meet a very nice couple from Tennessee. We spoke about our adult children and grandchildren, feeding the wildlife that ventures onto our properties. They informed us that they would be traveling to France once they left Williamsburg and would be staying and returning to France in the fall to go on a bike tour. They were very kind and well-educated. They helped me feel like there was more to our trip than Cancer.

Lori

> Enter by the narrow gate. For the gate is wide and the way is easy that leads to destruction, and those who enter by it are many. For the gate is narrow and the way is hard that leads to life, and those who find it are few.
>
> Matthew 7:13-14

Who was Jesus Speaking to? Analogous Scriptures suggest that it was His Disciples alone whom Jesus was teaching in this passage.

> And He strictly ordered them not to make Him known; And he went up on the mountain and called to him those whom he desired, and they came to him.
>
> Mark 3:12-13

> In these days he went out to the mountain to pray, and all night he continued in prayer to God; And when day came, he called his disciples and chose from them twelve, whom he named apostles.
>
> Luke 6:12-13

> Perceiving then that they were about to come and take him by force to make him king, Jesus withdrew again to the mountain by himself; So, when the crowd saw that Jesus was not there, nor his disciples, they themselves got into the boats and went to Capernaum, seeking Jesus.
>
> John 6:15-23

Jesus WAS NOT speaking to or about "irreligious" people here. Unlike our day, there were very few people who did not practice some form of religion. He did not live in a day or era when some claimed to be atheists. That was not His point. We need to go back to chapter 5 to get the answer.

> "For I tell you, unless your righteousness exceeds that of the scribes and Pharisees, you will never enter the kingdom of heaven."
>
> Matthew 5:20

Jesus was trying to tell us that those "religious" people who think they have it all figured out, those who have the answers, those who think that they are bound for heaven because they obey the law have got it all wrong

> "Not everyone who says to me, 'Lord, Lord,' will enter the kingdom of heaven, but the one who does the will of my Father who is in heaven. On that day many will say to me, 'Lord, Lord, did we not prophesy in your name, and cast out demons in your name, and do many mighty works

in your name?' And then will I declare to them, 'I never knew you; depart from me, you workers of lawlessness'"

> Matthew 7:21-23

Who is it that travels each of the 2 paths?
What qualities would we expect to see in one who is walking on the hard path? Who would you consider worthy of God's judgments? Would God, as some would argue, actually condemn someone to Hell, or is He the "forgiving" God that so many churches proclaim today?

> Righteousness and justice are the foundations of Your (God's) throne; steadfast love and faithfulness go before you.
>
> Psalm 89:14

God is indeed a God of love, but just like any house rests upon a foundation, God's love rests upon His justice. His love can never overrule His justice. Both must be served!

We ALL start out life on the wide or the easy path.

> No one is righteous, no, not one; no one understands; no one seeks for God. All have turned aside; together they have become worthless; no one does good, not even one.
>
> Romans 3:10-12

Righteousness is a conformity of heart and life to the law of God. Where is the man on earth that possesses it by nature? Where is the man whose deviations from this standard have not been innumerable?

> For all have sinned and fall short of the glory of God
> Romans 3:20

> The fool says in his heart, "There is no God." They are corrupt, they do abominable deeds, there is none who does good. The Lord looks down from heaven on the

children of man, to see if there are any who understand, who seek after God. They have all turned aside; together they have become corrupt; there is none who does good, not even one.

Psalm 14:1-3

Surely there is not a righteous man on earth who does good and never sins.

Ecclesiastes 7:20

All we like sheep have gone astray; we have turned—every one—to his own way; and the Lord has laid on him the iniquity of us all.

Isaiah 53:6

We have ALL chosen the wrong way—and it leads to death!

This passage describes an "All or Nothing" scenario. We cannot have it both ways where you constantly bounce back and forth between the paths, walking with one foot on the easy path and one foot on the hard path. WE CAN NOT have the easy life of the wide path and the rewards of the narrow path!

I remember a story about a concerned mother who thought perhaps her son was taking "Jesus" too far. The answer she got from his pastor was, "There is no such thing as too far where God is concerned. It was not too much for Him to sacrifice His Son for our own wickedness."

It is a choice! Jesus reiterates the words of Moses!

> I call heaven and earth to witness against you today, that I have set before you life and death, blessing and curse. Therefore choose life, that you and your offspring may live,
>
> Deuteronomy 30:19

"Thus says the Lord: Behold, I set before you the way of life and the way of death."

Jeremiah 21:8

The Wide and Narrow Gates

It is not an arbitrary choice. Both Moses in Deuteronomy and Jesus here in Matthew tell us which path to choose.

There are 2 Entrances

The Christian life MUST be entered into intentionally through repentance and faith!

> The time is fulfilled, and the kingdom of God is at hand; repent and believe in the gospel.
> Mark 1:15

Have you said a prayer at an altar call at some time in your life and believed you were saved? Do you believe you are a Christian because you attend Church every week? Or because you are involved in teaching Sunday School or helping with the offering, etc.? Are you a Christian because you were born and raised in a Christian home? Have you always been a Christian?

All of these are impossible by the way. You were not born repentant and believing! Jesus says to "enter" the narrow gate—not "stray" toward the narrow gate! Jesus says at the end of this passage that we must FIND the narrow gate!

The Wide Entrance (Pertaining to the gate—the legalism of the Pharisees):

The wide gate is our natural inclination.
We are guilty of Original sin.
We have inherited Adam's sin.
The wide gate is in plain view.
The wide gate provides easy access.
The wide gate is easy to open,
The wide gate might be left standing open already.

The Narrow Entrance:
The narrow gate requires change.
The narrow gate must be found (requires effort).

The Beatitudes are a picture of Kingdom Citizens, salt and light, the characteristics of believers as compared to the culture at large. It is an ascending line from commencement to completion. True Christianity is "Poor in spirit", "Mourns", "Meek", "Hungers and thirsts for righteousness", "Merciful", and "Pure in heart" (Notice the growth in the life of a true believer as the Christian life progresses from vs. 2 through vs. 12)

"Peace-making" is "Persecuted for righteousness's sake." We will "Rejoice and be glad." This is the life that Christ wants to give us—the kind of life that is evident if we are on the hard path.

There are 2 Paths

There are only 2 roads here—the road to salvation and everything else.

Islam, Buddhism, Mormonism, etc. all follow the wide road to destruction.

Contrary to popular culture that tells us there are many roads to heaven—there is only ONE path to salvation.

> "I am the way the truth and the life. NO ONE comes to the father but through me!"
>
> John 14:6

The Wide Road and The Easy Path to Salvation; The Gospel presentation of the purpose-driven life offers a 2 Step Salvation false salvation:

Step 1: Believe.

Believe that God loves you and made you for a purpose. Believe that God has chosen you to have a relationship with Jesus who died on the Cross for you. Believe that no matter what you've done God wants to forgive you.

Believe in Jesus—Which Jesus though? Should you believe in the

Jesus of the Mormons, the prophet Jesus of Islam, the created Jesus of the Jehovah's Witnesses, the meek and mild Jesus who loves everyone and wouldn't dare send anyone to Hell much less teach about such a place?

Step 2: Receive—again—a false salvation.

Receive Jesus into your life as Lord and Savior. Receive His forgiveness for your sins. Bow your head and say the sinner's prayer. You will be told that if you sincerely meant that prayer, you are among the family of God.

But, did you mean it when you said that prayer? Did you mean it because you're scared? Did you mean it because you want to stay out of Hell? Or, did you mean it because you understand the offense of your sins to a Holy and Righteous God?

This is a false gospel and one not to be found anywhere in Scripture. Where is the repentance? Where is the Gospel? Where is our sin? Where is the wrath of God? We are wretched, miserable, sinful creatures who deserve to die and go to Hell, and unless we repent of our sin and are aware of the fact that we deserve to die and be crushed under the weight of the Holiness and Majesty of God then WE DON'T GET IT!

This is the Hard Path to Salvation.

James Montgomery Boice pointed out that many of those who preach the Gospel these days are out of step with Jesus in this matter. Although they preach a gospel, they make it sound easy to become a Christian. It is difficult because we want to follow our own lives and worship a god who will bless it. We want God to be an extension of our lives and not eradication of our lives!

Satan taunts us. Our "old nature" doesn't want to die. Why should we die to our old ways? Aren't there many people who are on the wide path? Surely they can't all be wrong! Isn't it likely that we are too "narrow" in our interpretation of the Christian life?

The Christian life must be lived purposefully. Jesus tells us that there is a specific "way" to the Christian life. There is a lifestyle involved in the Christian life! We look again to the Beatitudes:

True Christianity is "Poor in spirit," "Mourns," "Meek," "Hungers and thirsts for righteousness," "Merciful," is "Pure in heart."

The Greek from which the word "hard" is derived is almost always translated in a way that means "persecution." So, in essence, this is what Jesus says in this passage. Those who enter into my kingdom enter it through a narrow gate and live a life that is filled with hardship and persecution! In contrast, the gospel of our day says that if you have a hard life then you need Jesus so that your life will be easy and that you will not have persecution in your life.

Paul says however in 2 Timothy 3:12 that all who desire to live a Godly life SHALL BE PERSECUTED.

> "Blessed are those who are persecuted for righteousness sake, for theirs is the Kingdom of Heaven. Blessed are you when others revile you and persecute you and utter all kinds of evil against you on my account! Rejoice and be glad, for your reward is in Heaven, for so they persecuted the prophets before you."
>
> Matthew 5:10-12

We should expect to be ridiculed as Christ was ridiculed, hated as He was hated, and sometimes, killed as He was killed. It is important to note here that the persecution comes because of our righteousness in Christ. It does not count if you are just a mean nasty person (Grinch) who deserves persecution!

> "Behold, I am sending you out as sheep in the midst of wolves, so be wise as serpents and innocent as doves. Beware of men, for they will deliver you over to courts and flog you in their synagogues, and you will be dragged before governors and kings for my sake, to bear witness before them and the Gentiles."
>
> Matthew 10:16-18

The Wide and Narrow Gates

"Brother will deliver brother over to death, and the father his child, and children will rise against parents and have them put to death, and you will be hated by all for my name's sake. But the one who endures to the end will be saved."

Matthew 10:21-22

"Then they will deliver you up to tribulation and put you to death, and you will be hated by all nations for my name's sake. And then many will fall away and betray one another and hate one another. And many false prophets will arise and lead many astray. And because lawlessness will be increased, the love of many will grow cold. But the one who endures to the end will be saved."

Matthew 24 9-13

There are 2 Groups of people

The many:

We believe that most people are good and only a few will go to Hell. We believe that because we are among the many that we are on the path to life. Adolf Hitler, Benito Mussolini, Pol-Pot, and Charles Manson, to name a few. Because we don't believe in the "original sin" of Adam, we believe that everybody is born good and turns evil.

> Therefore, just as sin came into the world through one man, and death through sin, and so death spread to all men because all sinned.
>
> Romans 5:12

Adam, our federal head, sinned and ALL his posterity fell with him.

Most people believe that only a few people are going to Hell, we tend to judge our lives by our own standards instead of God's standards. We are "good" in our own eyes, so we are saved. We justify our lives with ideas like, "I try to live a good life," "I never killed anybody," and "I don't cheat on my wife." This is an upside-down theology and IT IS WRONG!

Look again at Romans 3:10-12 "No-one is righteous, no, not one; no one understands; no one seeks for God. All have turned aside; together they have become worthless; no one does good, not even one." We are in Active Rebellion. Not only are we born into sin and by nature travel the wide road, but we also act on that sin.

> And you were dead in the trespasses and sins in which you once walked, following the course of this world, following the prince of the power of the air, the spirit that is now at work in the sons of disobedience among whom we all once lived in the passions of our flesh, carrying out the desires of the body and the mind, and were by nature children of wrath, like the rest of mankind.
>
> Ephesians 2 1-3

The sad fact is many who sit in Church today are on the wide path to destruction and do not even know it. People who have bought into the lie of the "sinner's prayer."

> "Not everyone who says to me, 'Lord, Lord,' will enter the kingdom of heaven, but the one who does the will of my Father who is in heaven. On that day many will say to me, 'Lord, Lord, did we not prophesy in your name, and cast out demons in your name, and do many mighty works in your name?' And then will I declare to them, 'I never knew you; depart from me, you workers of lawlessness.'"
>
> Matthew 7:21-23

The Wide and Narrow Gates

The few:

This road is oftentimes lonely, especially when believers do not reach out to each other while on this road. The gate is already narrow and the road already hard and we seem to somehow find a way to shun each other as we travel this path.

Legalism and isolationism—we do not need to make the road any harder than it already is by being so critical of those who call on God in the name of Christ. We need to stop with the division and cruelty most of today's "Christians" carry around and just learn to be brothers and sisters in Christ. Let Him do the work of their faith relationship with Him and we just need to be there to support that work in prayer.

> "For the gate is narrow and the way is hard that leads to life, and those who find it are few."
>
> Matthew 7:14

There are only 2 Destinations

Destruction:

> But as for the cowardly, the faithless, the detestable, as for murderers, the sexually immoral, sorcerers, idolaters, and all liars, their portion will be in the lake that burns with fire and sulfur, which is the second death.
>
> Revelation 21:8

And Life:

Endurance the truth is evidence of our salvation

> "But the one who endures to the end will be saved."
>
> Matthew 24:13

The Christ in my Cancer

In many ways, it's like "running a race" or fighting in a boxing ring.

> For I am already being poured out as a drink offering, and the time of my departure has come. I have fought the good fight, I have finished the race, I have kept the faith. Henceforth there is laid up for me the crown of righteousness, which the Lord, the righteous judge, will award to me on that Day, and not only to me but also to all who have loved his appearing.
>
> 2 Timothy 4:6-8

We are to be active, not passive, in our faith.

> Examine yourselves, to see whether you are in the faith. Test yourselves. Or do you not realize this about yourselves, that Jesus Christ is in you?—unless indeed you fail to meet the test!
>
> 2 Corinthians 13:5

What are you going to do about this? It's a simple choice:

The Narrow Gate & the Hard Road lead to LIFE
The Wide Gate & The Easy Road lead to DEATH

A decision needs to be made. If you are simply going to sit and listen without taking action based upon what Scripture is telling us, then you have just wasted your time. ACT!

> "Do not lay up for yourselves treasures on earth, where moth and rust destroy and where thieves break in and steal, but lay up for yourselves treasures in heaven, where neither moth nor rust destroys and where thieves do not break in and steal. For where your treasure is, there your heart will be also.

The Wide and Narrow Gates

No one can serve two masters, for either he will hate the one and love the other, or he will be devoted to the one and despise the other. You cannot serve God and money."

> Matthew 6:19-21, 24

You make known to me the path of life . . .

> Psalm 16:11a

Where does He do this? Scriptures!

Jesus said to him, "I am the way and the truth and the life. No one comes to the Father except through Me"

> John 14:5

By the straight gate, we understand humility, repentance, and renunciation of the world, through poverty in spirit. The wide gate is the self-righteousness of the Pharisees or the spurious riches of piety which is combined with the service of possessions. Similarly, the narrow way is the prosecution of those spiritual attainments described in the seven beatitudes; while the broad way indicates that corruption in doctrine and life, which, passing from one extreme to the other, renders the way so wide and ill-defined. The contrast between the goal of these two ways is exceedingly significant.

In one case, it is life: in the other, destruction. First, as a matter of inward experience, then of outward fact, and, lastly, of eternal destiny (rest and unrest, deliverance and destruction, salvation, and condemnation). The figurative language of this passage is closely connected with what precedes the relation of Christians to their fellow men. You must devote yourselves to others, not according to the measure which they demand at your hand, but according as you would have them do to you. You are not to follow the multitude on the broad way, but to seek with the few, the elect, the strait gate, in order to knock at the door of the kingdom of heaven. Such is the transition from the injunction of what we are to seek, to that of what we are to avoid. Test yourself to see if you be in the faith.

Repent because you know and agree with God that you are a wretched sinner both in nature and in deed and that you deserve the wrath that a Holy and Righteous God MUST give to those who sin in order to satisfy His justice!

Repentance is self-abhorrence. Being so utterly sick of yourself that you would do anything to get away from your sinful self. Repentance is recognizing that everything in you is filthy and wretched and DOES NOT deserve to be in the presence of a Holy God and you cry out to the only one who can make you different!

Repentance is placing your faith in the Jesus of the Scriptures—the God-Man, the one who was born of a virgin, the one who performed miracles, the one who died on the cross, the one who rose again on the third day, the one who is coming again to judge the living and the dead, the one who was the author of creation, the one who is an answer your sin problem.

Faith in, not just the name, but in the person and work of Jesus Christ. When you understand that, you understand what it means to find the narrow gate and to walk the hard road! If you do not understand your sin in this manner, then my friend are on the wide path and are lost!

CHAPTER 5

The Christian Life on the Hard Road

Belhurst Castle, Seneca Lake NY:

What an amazing time. We stayed in the original castle, where the modern niceties did not exist when the place was built. Our room was on the third floor, with no elevator or air conditioning and I am glad it was so as we had a great opportunity to enjoy the architecture, stained glass windows, etc. I felt like a Scottish princess walking through the castle as we discovered new rooms and woodwork throughout our days. The grounds brought such peace and calm to my weary soul.

Lori

Characteristics of the Christian Life

There are certain characteristics that Christ talks about here that give us an indication of the character of the true Christian life. A Christian "Worldview." We must learn to develop a "New" Christian worldview and abandon our carnal, earthly worldview. We must live our lives focused on our future Heavenly reward rather than our present worldly reward. (Something which I have had a hard view of recently).

Living for something other than ourselves

We must come to a point where we no longer live our lives for ourselves, but for something greater as defined in Scripture. We must understand that this IS NOT our best life now, which is a heretical viewpoint and one that leads us to our own destruction. We need to adopt a Christ-like life that is lived in sacrifice and devoted to others. We need to understand at the outset what Jesus means by the term "Blessed" if we are to properly understand this passage. We also need a proper biblical understanding of the term "Holy" if we are to walk this path as Christ commands.

From these sentences, which commence verses 3–10, we gather what blessedness Jesus has in view—that of the kingdom of Messiah.

Jesus declares those who are to be blessed are those whom the men of the world would hold to be most unhappy. He designates by those term circumstances which, to those looking merely at the outside, would appear far from enviable, and traits of character running directly contrary to a carnal worldview.

These sentences contain many paradoxes.

> Webster's Dictionary defines a paradox as "a statement that seems to say two opposite things but in truth are both true."[5]

Nothing New!

Although these statements of Christ run directly counter to the carnal prejudices of His contemporaries, Jesus' words contain nothing entirely new or unknown, since all these beatitudes are based upon passages from the Old Testament.

> For thus says the One who is high and lifted up, who inhabits eternity, whose name is Holy: I dwell in the high and holy place, and also with him who is of a contrite and lowly spirit,

---

5 Webster's Dictionary: https://www.merriam-webster.com/dictionary/ Viewed October 11, 2022

to revive the spirit of the lowly, and to revive the heart of the contrite.

Isaiah 57:15

The Spirit of the Lord God is upon me, because the Lord has anointed me to bring good news to the poor; he has sent me to bind up the brokenhearted, to proclaim liberty to the captives, and the opening of the prison to those who are bound

Isaiah 61:1-3

Come, O children, listen to me; I will teach you the fear of the Lord. What man is there who desires life and loves many days, that he may see good? Keep your tongue from evil and your lips from speaking deceit. Turn away from evil and do good; seek peace and pursue it. The eyes of the Lord are toward the righteous and his ears toward their cry. The face of the Lord is against those who do evil, to cut off the memory of them from the earth. When the righteous cry for help, the Lord hears and delivers them out of all their troubles. The Lord is near to the brokenhearted and saves the crushed in spirit. Many are the afflictions of the righteous, but the Lord delivers him out of them all.

Psalm 34:11-19

Truly God is good to Israel, to those who are pure in heart.

Psalm 73:1

Those who were full have hired themselves out for bread, but those who were hungry have ceased to hunger. The barren has borne seven, but she who has many children is forlorn

1 Samuel 2:5

The sacrifices of God are a broken spirit; a broken and contrite heart, O God, you will not despise.

Psalm 51:17

The heart of the wise is in the house of mourning, but the heart of fools is in the house of mirth.

Ecclesiastes 7:4

It is worthy of notice, that, like the beatitudes of Jesus, Psalm 1 describes a corresponding state of mind, and admonishes believers to cherish and seek such a spiritual attitude. Blessed is the man who walks not in the counsel of the wicked, nor stands in the way of sinners, nor sits in the seat of scoffers, but his delight is in the law of the Lord, and on his law, he meditates day and night. He is like a tree planted by streams of water that yields its fruit in its season, and its leaf does not wither. In all that he does, he prospers. The wicked are not so but are like chaff that the wind drives away. Therefore, the wicked will not stand in the judgment, nor sinners in the congregation of the righteous; for the Lord knows the way of the righteous, but the way of the wicked will perish.

A Christian is "Poor In Spirit"

This describes those who feel spiritually poor, and hence realize their deep and inexpressible want of the Spirit, and long for the true religion given by the Holy Spirit. Hence the expression does not imply poverty of spirit about the man and is much less an indication of intellectual poverty. The idea that it refers to external poverty, voluntarily chosen, or to a vow of voluntary poverty, as some of the older Roman Catholic commentators imagine deserves no further notice.

The original Greek in this passage indicates that "Poor in Spirit" is a primary and essential characteristic of Christianity. It is indeed true that the expression bears special reference to the poor and needy of the Old Testament as found in Isaiah 61:1 and 66:2 and indicates a spiritual longing for true righteousness.

The Christian Life on the Hard Road

A Christian "Mourns"

We must not imply that the term "mourns" as used in this context means that a Christian mourns on account of his or her sin alone, nor does it indicate sadness and sorrow in general.

The state of mind that this refers to is explained by the "poverty in spirit" from which it springs, as described in the previous verse, and tends toward hungering and thirsting after righteousness.

2 Corinthians 7:10 For godly grief produces a repentance that leads to salvation without regret, whereas worldly grief produces death.

This "mourning" includes not only mourning on account of sin, but also on account of its consequences; more particularly, it is the expression of a state of mind when the world, with its possessions and pleasures, is no longer capable of satisfying, gladdening, or comforting.

From the beginning of this passage, the objective Christ was speaking to was the final righteousness of the kingdom of heaven and those who will occupy it. Hence, this "mourning" implies spiritual mourning and divine sorrow in opposition to the sorrow of the world. This, then, is a state of mind that is IN God through His Holy Spirit, FROM God in His blessings, and FOR God to His glory.

A Christian is "Meek"

> Webster's Dictionary defines the word meek as "having or showing a quiet and gentle nature: not wanting to fight or argue with other people" and "enduring injury (persecution) with patience and without resentment."[6]

We will undoubtedly endure "suffering" at the hands of "this present age" for our decision to walk the "hard road". Meekness then, in context, means that we are to endure this persecution with Godly

---

6   Webster's Dictionary: https://www.merriam-webster.com/dictionary/ Viewed October 11, 2022

patience just as Christ prayed for those who persecuted Him.

> "Father forgive them for they know not what they do . . ."
> but the rulers scoffed at Him
>
> Luke 23:34-35

> But the meek shall inherit the land and delight themselves in abundant peace.
>
> Psalm 37:11

Meekness then refers to those who suffer in love or love in patience; those who, in the strength of love, boldly yet meekly, meekly yet boldly, bear injustice, and thereby conquer. Meekness though does not mean that we are to be weak, or pushovers and are not necessarily to allow others to "walk all over us".

The word "meek" from the original language was used to describe "reigning in a stallion". It is the idea of a horse being controlled by a bit and bridle. The horse "chooses" to submit to authority. Meekness then, in this context, is power restrained.

Again, we need to look to the life of Christ to understand the difference between "meekness" and "weakness."

> "Take my yoke upon you, and learn from me, for I am gentle and lowly in heart, and you will find rest for your souls," as compared to Matthew 28:18 where Jesus says, "All authority in heaven and on earth has been given unto Me."
>
> Matthew 11:29

Note the present tense in the words of Christ. Christ HAS all of the authority that ever was, and yet says of Himself that He IS, at the same time, gentle and lowly in heart! We are to model that same meekness in our own lives if we are to walk the hard and narrow road.

The Christian Life on the Hard Road

A Christian is to "Hunger and Thirst" for righteousness

Hunger and thirst in this passage indicate a desire so intense that it is painful. Hunger and thirst are innate and natural impulses God built into everyone and every living thing in the world has this. God put it there not because he wants us to suffer, but because He doesn't want us to die. Hunger and thirst are primal instincts that drive us to go and get food and water regardless of the cost to ourselves!

The same should be applied to righteousness. Those who are traveling the hard road in pursuit of the Christian life are to be as driven by the need for God's righteousness as we are by the need for food so that we don't starve.

In other words, spiritual starvation should be as painful and repulsive to us as it would be for us to be deprived of food unto starvation. The body becomes emaciated and will eventually digest the very structure of our bodies in a vain attempt to survive!

But what is the righteousness that Christ speaks of in this passage?

> ...Noah was a righteous man, blameless in his generation...
>
> Genesis 6:9

> "When you reap the harvest of your land, you shall not reap your field right up to its edge, neither shall you gather the gleanings after your harvest. And you shall not strip your vineyard bare, neither shall you gather the fallen grapes of your vineyard. You shall leave them for the poor and for the sojourner: I am the Lord your God. You shall not steal; you shall not deal falsely; you shall not lie to one another. You shall not swear by my name falsely, and so profane the name of your God: I am the Lord. You shall not oppress your neighbor or rob him. The wages of a hired worker shall not remain with you all night until the morning. You shall not curse the deaf or put a stumbling block before the blind, but you shall

fear your God: I am the Lord. You shall do no injustice in court. You shall not be partial to the poor or defer to the great, but in righteousness shall you judge your neighbor. You shall not go around as a slanderer among your people, and you shall not stand up against the life of your neighbor: I am the Lord. You shall not hate your brother in your heart, but you shall reason frankly with your neighbor, lest you incur sin because of him. You shall not take vengeance or bear a grudge against the sons of your own people, but you shall love your neighbor as yourself: I am the Lord."

Leviticus 19:9-18

And it will be righteousness for us, if we are careful to do all this commandment (the 10 commandments) before the Lord our God, as he has commanded us.

Deuteronomy 6:25

For our sake he made Him to be sin who knew no sin, so that in Him we might become the righteousness of God.

2 Corinthians 5:21d

A Christian is to be "Merciful"

If the meek are to bear the injustice of the world, then the merciful bravely address themselves to the wants of the world.

These are acts that do not necessarily require the sacrifice of finances, material possessions, or our "stuff," but are instead sacrifices of the heart, time, strength, rest, comfort, etc.

The assistance to the sick and prisoners is not in their healing and release, which few could render, but in visitation and comfort, sympathy and attention, love and compassion which all of us can bestow. It is done in faith and humility and is the product of divine grace, for charity is the daughter of faith, and faith is the gift of the Holy Spirit, who unites us with Christ.

The Christian Life on the Hard Road

"Faith without works (Mercy) is dead." THIS is our clearest proof that we are truly saved and stems from a heart of compassion!

These are the outward indications of our salvation—Works though are not how we achieve salvation, but instead are the "fruits" of our salvation and without these outward fruits in evidence, there is likely no inward change to the heart and consequently no true salvation.

> "For I was hungry and you gave me food, I was thirsty and you gave me drink, I was a stranger and you welcomed me, I was naked and you clothed me, I was sick and you visited me, I was in prison and you came to me".
>
> Matthew 25:35

> Is it not to share your bread with the hungry and bring the homeless poor into your house; when you see the naked, to cover him, and not to hide yourself from your own flesh
>
> Isaiah 58:7

> What good is it, my brothers, if someone says he has faith but does not have works? Can that faith save him? If a brother or sister is poorly clothed and lacking in daily food, and one of you says to them, Go in peace, be warmed and filled, without giving them the things needed for the body, what good is that? So also faith by itself, if it does not have works, is dead.
>
> James 2:14-17

> But be doers of the word, and not hearers only, deceiving yourselves. For if anyone is a hearer of the word and not a doer, he is like a man who looks intently at his natural face in a mirror. For he looks at himself and goes away and at once forgets what he was like. But the one who looks into the perfect law, the law of liberty, and

perseveres, being no hearer who forgets but a doer who Acts, he will be blessed in his doing.

James 1:22-2

By this we know love, that he laid down his life for us, and we ought to lay down our lives for the brothers. But if anyone has the world's goods and sees his brother in need, yet closes his heart against him, how does God's love abide in him? Little children, let us not love in word or talk but in deed and in truth.

1 John 3:16-18

"This is my commandment, that you love one another as I have loved you. Greater love has no one than this, that someone lay down his life for his friends".

John 15:12-14

A Christian is to be "Pure in Heart"

This refers to the righteousness that is the ruling principle of the heart and inner life that defines every Christian. The purity of the heart consists in that steady direction of the soul toward the divine life which excludes every other object from the homage of the heart. Hence "inward moral integrity" is not sufficient, irrespective of the fact, that such integrity bears reference to an external moral standard. Our Lord, however, does not require absolute purity; else He would have said: They behold God. The term refers to a life pure in the inmost tendency and direction of the heart because it is entirely set upon what is eternally and absolutely pure. Hence it applies to walking in the Spirit, to a life of increased sanctification, and to being born of God. When the inmost heart is pure, its outward actions of our lives will also be pure. The inner life will ever manifest itself more and more clearly in the actions that are taken toward others as a result of increasing righteousness.

"Hear and understand: it is not what goes into the mouth that defiles a person, but what comes out of the mouth... Do you not see that whatever goes into the mouth passes into the stomach and is expelled? But what comes out of the mouth proceeds from the heart, and this defiles a person. For out of the heart come evil thoughts, murder, adultery, sexual immorality, theft, false witness, slander. These are what defile a person."

Matthew 15:10,11,17-20

"For out of the abundance of the heart the mouth speaks. The good person out of his good treasure brings forth good, and the evil person out of his evil treasure brings forth evil. I tell you, on the day of judgment people will give account for every careless word they speak, for by your words you will be justified, and by your words you will be condemned."

Matthew 12:34b-37

Christians are to be "Peacemakers"

Not merely meaning to be peaceful, but being peacemakers implies that action is required. It denotes the efforts made by the "pure in heart" on behalf of the Kingdom of Heaven, alluding more to the "messengers of peace" under the New Testament with the power and truth of the Word to which we bear witness.

It seems obvious that Jesus thinks of peacemaking as all the acts of love by which we try to overcome the enmity between us and other people. And if we ask for specifics, he gives two examples.

We, as Christians, are to be in prayer for those who persecute us. We are also told that if we are indeed "sons of God" we are to love these same persecutors as we love ourselves.

Matthew 5:43-46; "You have heard that it was said, 'You shall love your neighbor and hate your enemy.' But I say to you, Love your enemies and pray for those who persecute you, so that you may be sons of your Father who is in heaven. For he makes his sun rise on the evil and on the good, and sends rain on the just and on the unjust. For if you love those who love you, what reward do you have? Do not even the tax collectors do the same?"

We are also to make the extra effort to be the first to reach out to repair the broken relationships that exist between ourselves and others with whom we have strife.

> "And if you greet only your brothers, what more are you doing than others? Do not even the Gentiles do the same?"
>
> Matthew 5:47

Are we able to humble ourselves and cast away the pride that insists that we are "right" in our anger with others when we feel that we have been "wronged"?

Do we seek out those who have offended us in some way, or do we go out of our way to avoid those with whom we have had a conflict in the past, or are we the first to approach those same people and "put forth the hand of forgiveness"? When we see that person walking along the same sidewalk that we are on, do we approach them in humility, putting aside our damaged feelings in an attempt to make "peace" with them, or do we cross to the other side of the street or hide from them at the first opportunity so that we do not have to confront the issues that divide us?

Peacemaking tries to build bridges with people. It does not want the animosity to remain. It wants reconciliation. It wants harmony. And so it tries to show what may be the only courtesy the enemy will tolerate, namely, a greeting. The peacemaker looks the enemy right in the eye and says, "Good morning, John." And he says it with a longing for peace in his heart, not with a phony gloss of politeness to cover his anger.

In other words, we must love peace and work for peace. We must pray for our enemies, do good to them, greet them, and long for the barriers between us to be overcome.

The Christian Life on the Hard Road

We have all heard the analogy that says, "it is easier to attract ants with honey than it is with vinegar," and so it is as well with the Gospel. If we desire that others be open to the salvation offered through the Gospel of Jesus Christ, we should expect that the greatest results begin with the heart of a peacemaker.

Christians should expect to be "persecuted" for righteousness's sake, to be "reviled" and have their character maligned for the sake of Christ.

Persecuted, from the Greek, Dioko, means to follow or press hard after, literally to pursue as one does a fleeing enemy. It means to chase, harass, vex, and pressure and was used for chasing down criminals. Dioko speaks of an intensity of effort leading to a pursuit with earnestness and diligence in order to lay hold of and oppress or harass the "blessed".

> "And this is the judgment: the light has come into the world, and people loved the darkness rather than the light because their works were evil. For everyone who does wicked things hates the light and does not come to the light, lest his works should be exposed."
>
> What does Jesus say light does to the deeds of men who love darkness? His light in you and through you will expose the evil nature of their deeds! When His "righteousness" lights up your life you will be persecuted by the "light haters".
>
> John 3:19-20

You might naturally think that the unsaved world will persecute us because we are light and they are darkness. Therefore, they hate us because the light in us exposes their evil deeds, and while that is true, some of us are caught off guard when we are persecuted by others in the church.

Matthew 7:21-23; Not everyone in the church is a genuine believer but are not only professors of the faith, knowing the words

The Christ in my Cancer

to say and the things to do that imitate true Christianity. When they encounter a real, radical convert of Christ, they are taken aback and this sets the scene for persecution in one form or another, and although it can be very subtle, it is still very painful.

Think about who were the most persistent persecutors of our Lord... the religious community, those who knew a lot of Bible knowledge but did not know the truth Himself. Times may have changed but have men's hearts?

Why are we so surprised that the most vicious attacks will come from those who are in the same church? Who were the first persecutors of the newborn church in Jerusalem? Was it not the religious folk again? They are the very Jews who Jesus had presented Himself as King, but they would not have Him.

D. Martin Lloyd-Jones wrote, "By whom are the righteous persecuted? You will find as you go through the Scriptures, and as you study the history of the Church, that the persecution is not confined to the world. Some of the most grievous persecution has been suffered by the righteous at the hands of the Church herself, and at the hands of religious people. It has often come from nominal Christians. Take our Lord Himself. Who were His chief persecutors? The Pharisees and scribes and the doctors of the Law! The first Christians, too, were persecuted most bitterly of all by the Jews. Then read the history of the Church, and watch it in the Roman Catholic persecution of some of those men in the Middle Ages who had seen the pure truth and were trying to live it out quietly. How they were persecuted by nominal, religious people! That was also the story of the Puritan Fathers. This is the teaching of the Bible, and it has been substantiated by the history of the Church, that the persecution may come, not from the outside but from within. There are ideas of Christianity far removed from the New Testament which are held by many and which cause them to persecute those who are trying in sincerity and truth to follow the Lord Jesus Christ along the narrow way. You may well find it in your own personal experience. I have often been told by converts that they get much more opposition from supposedly Christian people than they do from the man of the world outside, who is often glad to see them changed and wants to know something about it. Formal Christianity is often the greatest enemy of the pure faith."omething about it. Formal Christianity is often the greatest enemy of the pure faith."[7]

> Webster's Dictionary definition of Truth: "the body of true statements and propositions; the property of being in accord with fact or reality."[8]

Remember and understand the sequence of the Christian life as it progresses through the 9 stages of the beatitudes.

First, following salvation, God takes away our heart of stone and begins to replace it with a heart of flesh that is "Poor in Spirit", leading us to be "Mournful" over not only our individual sin, but also over the sin of the entire world. We are made "Meek" in this understanding of our sinful nature and its disregard for the holiness of God, thus developing in us a "Hunger and Thirst" for God's righteousness instead of our own. It is this righteousness, God's righteousness, that results in "Mercy" where others are concerned. A "Pure Heart" will cause us to be "Peacemakers" just as clouds bring rain or lightning causes thunder. The one is a natural result of the other and one cannot exist without the other. In the end, this new "Heart of Flesh" that God gives us will result in our persecution from the darkness of the world in which we live, and most often this persecution comes from those whom we least expect it—the unsaved church. It is this "Persecution for Righteousness Sake" that is ultimately the "Test" of a true faith in Jesus Christ and a True Salvation Experience. (Ezekiel 36:25-27; 2 Corinthians 13:5)

---

7 https://www.monergism.com/persecuted-righteousness-sake-christian-and-persecution-d-martyn-lloyd-jones-1899-1981. Viewed October 11, 2022
8 Webster's Dictionary: https://www.merriam-webster.com/dictionary/ Viewed October 11, 2022

The rewards of these character traits are not to be missed

The Kingdom of Heaven belongs to the "Poor in Spirit." The "Mournful" shall be comforted.

The "Meek" shall inherit the Earth. Those who "Hunger and Thirst" for righteousness shall be satisfied. The "Merciful" shall receive mercy in turn. The "Pure in Heart" shall see God. The "Peacemakers" shall be called sons of God.

The Kingdom of Heaven belongs to those who are "Persecuted" for righteousness' sake.

We are to rejoice and be glad as we suffer the hardships that will beset us as we walk the "Hard Road" of Matthew 7:13-14. We need to always keep the goal in sight.

In the end—our reward is GREAT! Our reward is LIFE!

There is a single passage of Scripture that perhaps sums this up best. If I could ask you to memorize one passage of Scripture to help when the hard road seems unusually hard it might be this one from Ezekiel.

> "I will sprinkle clean water on you, and you shall be clean from all your uncleanness's, and from all your idols I will cleanse you. And I will give you a new heart, and a new spirit I will put within you. And I will remove the heart of stone from your flesh and give you a heart of flesh. And I will put my Spirit within you and cause you to walk in my statutes and be careful to obey my rules."
>
> Ezekiel 36:25-27

CHAPTER 6

Guilt, Grace, and Gratitude

Ocean City New Jersey:

Wonderful trip, probably the best trip of the summer. The first 3 days we were without hot water (needed a new gas water heater). Everyone was SO wonderful, from the owner to the folks upstairs to the plumber who fixed the heater. The folks we met could not have been more friendly or outgoing to us. The condo we stayed at was very nice, and modest. (The condo was only a block from the beach and was also only about 20 blocks from the boardwalk.) I am in constant AWE of God's creation, the vastness of the ocean, and how it seems to touch the sky, filled with living creatures and small grains of sand. Here I can lose my thoughts and refresh my heart. While there, our eldest son and his family stayed overnight. We enjoyed the boardwalk as we got ice cream for my granddaughter. Great family time. Scottie had the chance to feed our newest grandson and let him take a nap on his chest as he did with our own kids when they were young.

Lori

And you were dead in the trespasses and sins in which you once walked, following the course of this world, following the prince of the power of the air, the spirit that is now at work in the sons of disobedience—among whom we all once lived in the passions of our flesh, carrying out the desires of the body and the mind, and were by nature children of wrath, like the rest of mankind. But God, being rich in mercy, because of the great love with which he loved us, even when we were dead in our trespasses, made us alive together with Christ—by grace, you have been saved—and raised us up with him and seated us with him in the heavenly places in Christ Jesus, so that in the coming ages he might show the immeasurable riches of his grace in kindness toward us in Christ Jesus. For by grace you have been saved through faith. And this is not your own doing; it is the gift of God, not a result of works, so that no one may boast. For we are his workmanship, created in Christ Jesus for good works, which God prepared beforehand, that we should walk in them.

Ephesians 2:1-10

What is Grace?

For that matter—What is justice? What is mercy?

In its simplest form justice means "getting what we deserve." Be very careful when you cry out for justice. You may just get what you are asking for! And in truth, NONE of us really wants God's justice. We speak from ignorance and hatred of God when we demand this "worldly justice." Mercy means "we DO NOT get what we deserve." Grace means "we get what we DO NOT deserve." Guilt, Grace, and Gratitude. The 3G's of the Gospel. If we do not fully understand and embrace our Guilt, we cannot appreciate God's Grace. If we do not live our lives in Gratitude to Him, we do not understand His Grace OR our Guilt.

Amazing Grace: (The one song I want to be sung at my funeral—preferably with bagpipes) was written in 1772. The words for this beloved song were borne from the heart, mind, and experiences of the Englishman John Newton. Having lived through a troubled life, Newton spent years fighting against authority, going so far as trying to desert the Royal Navy in his twenties. Later, abandoned by his

Guilt, Grace, and Gratitude

crew in West Africa, he was forced to be a servant to a slave trader. Upon his return, Newton became a slave ship master, bringing slaves from Africa to England over multiple trips. He, admittedly, treated the slaves abhorrently. In 1754, after becoming violently ill at sea, Newton abandoned the slave trade and his life as a slave trader and wholeheartedly devoted his life to God's service. Ordained as an Anglican priest in 1764, Newton penned over 280 Hymns including the words to the beloved hymn, Amazing Grace.

And now, we see how lyrics like, "I once was lost, but now am found, was blind but now I see.", "Through many dangers, toils, and snares I have already come." and, "Tis grace hath brought me safe thus far, and grace will lead me home," carry a much deeper meaning than a sinner's mere gratitude. The heartache and pain from Newtons' tumultuous past most assuredly played a part in the writing of this Hymn that has blessed Christians now for more than 200 years.

He finally understood his own Guilt, which led to his understanding of the Amazing Grace God displayed in redeeming him AND he most certainly understood the Gratitude that comes from such understanding.

It is my prayer that as we each face the trials that come our way each day, we too can see the magnificent Grace that God poured out on sinners and sing along with John Newton. 'Twas grace that taught my heart to fear and grace my fears relieved. How precious did that grace appear the hour I first believed.

Twice in our passage, Paul tells us that we "have been saved by Grace." Note the verbiage in this passage, "We HAVE BEEN saved by Grace!" Not only is this phrase "past tense," meaning that we have already been saved by God's Grace, but it also means that this "saving" was a passive act on our part. We WERE saved, we DID NOT save ourselves!

Ours is a condition of great bankruptcy, great ruin. Grace overturns our ruined condition in such a way that we are forced to confess that everything we have, everything that we are, every single blessing that we have received, the reality of forgiveness, hope, joy, and worship is ALL a result of God's Grace. From beginning to end, Grace is all the result of the undeserved and un-coerced favor of God!

Our Current Condition—Guilty

> And you were dead in the trespasses and sins in which you once walked, following the course of this world, following the prince of the power of the air, the spirit that is now at work in the sons of disobedience—among whom we all once lived in the passions of our flesh, carrying out the desires of the body and the mind, and were by nature children of wrath, like the rest of mankind" "We are darkened in our understanding, alienated from the life of God because of the ignorance that is in us, due to their hardness of heart. We have become callous and have given ourselves up to sensuality, greedy to practice every kind of impurity.
>
> Ephesians 2:1-3, 4:18-19

We are Spiritually Dead with a darkened Understanding: Wholly unable to understand spiritual realities, we simply cannot understand. God's truths simply "do not compute." Our worldview is one in which the material and the sensual represent the only reality that exists. What does daily life look like for you? Are your goals and desires filled with the material and sensual things the world would offer or are your goals and desires "in line" with Jesus Christ, the one who has been given ALL authority in Heaven and Earth?

We are alienated from God

Hinduism, Buddhism, Taoism, Shintoism, Judaism, Islam...

The list goes on and on... Religious faiths throughout the world, all of them seeking God, purpose, meaning, and truth. The overwhelming majority of humanity is seeking God and His truth, actively involved in the capricious search for understanding.

- 86% of the world's 7.8 billion people practice a faith of some kind.

Guilt, Grace, and Gratitude

- 73% of the world's 7.8 billion people practice one of the 5 most well-known faiths—Christianity, Judaism, Islam, Hinduism, and Buddhism.

This tells us that humans are by their very nature creatures designed for worship. It also tells us that without the divine guidance of a designer of that nature, we have no hope of finding the truth for ourselves.

Every single one of the numerous religions in the world offers salvation by works and works alone. It is in our own effort and sacrifices that we believe we can provide some sort of mercy and grace with God based on our own "Earthly Standard of Character," when most of us completely misunderstand that it is God's standards we are judged by. When it comes to true salvation, the world's religions completely miss the point. Salvation is from Jesus Christ and Him alone. It is not by our own effort or our own "works" that justifies us, but His own work on the cross that justifies us.

Those who are Spiritually Dead do not care at all that they are. It simply does not bother them that they are alienated from God, it would never occur to them that this would be a bad thing.

They are eager to live for their own selfish desires, chained to whatever their hunger dictates.

Not only blind and disinterested but captive to the curse of this world. Those who are morally captive are squeezed into the world's mold and coerced into certain ways of thinking, and acting that reflects the conventional wisdom of the world.

This is The Insanity of Man's Wisdom!

We don't form our opinions as righteously as we'd like, but rather as the world does. Their ready-made thoughts are in our newsfeeds, ripe for our picking. Right down to our preferred appearance, we are controlled by the preferences of the world around us.

It is our culture, the conventional wisdom of our world that squeezes us into its mold and removes the fallacy that we have "Free Will." If our world says an unborn child is just a "mass of tissue," we say in unison "it's a woman's right to choose"! If our world says that sensuality—not just sexual sensuality, but ALL flesh-driven sensuality is just "The Empowerment of Hedonism," then we hail in unison—"if it feels good, let's do it."

The thing that is the icing over ALL the "Wisdom of the Age" is that the forces of our enemy are behind it all. Captive to "The Prince of the Power of the Air", the rulers, authorities, and cosmic powers over this present darkness. Captive to the forces of evil in heavenly places!

"We all once lived in the passions of our flesh, carrying out the desires of the body and the mind" Look around—enough said.

In our spiritually dead, blind, and captive state, we do not fight against the forces arrayed against us. On the contrary, we welcome them with open arms into our lives.

We derive great pleasure in following the fashions and trends of society.

We delight in surrendering to and surrounding ourselves with those things which either delight us at the moment or cover the pain of insecurity as we find our worth in our stuff!

We are Condemned

> "For if we go on sinning deliberately after receiving the knowledge of the truth, there no longer remains a sacrifice for sins, but a fearful expectation of judgment, and a fury of fire that will consume the adversaries—For we know him who said, 'Vengeance is mine; I will repay.' And again, "The Lord will judge his people." It is a fearful thing to fall into the hands of the living God."
>
> Hebrews 10:26-27, 30-31

Our condition is that we are all quite simply RUINED—bankrupt, corrupt and corruptible, condemned, guilty as charged, and waiting for execution!

Humanity is so spiritually blind to God and His truth that our "seeking" will always revert to the physical rather than the spiritual as is our fallen nature. It is the core of the Great Lie. We focus our "seeking" on all those things that we can do ourselves and hinge our security on how well we perform those tasks.

Left to our own devices we would never look for the truth in a God that has already done all the work and simply says, "Come."

It is an affront to our pride!

I am NOT corrupt! I am NOT blind! I am NOT perverted and twisted in my every thought!

In the end, it is our pride that blinds us to Him and leaves us spiritually dead.

We CAN NOT see Him because we REFUSE to see Him!

Our Hope—Grace

If we were to receive Justice, we would already be languishing in the eternal wrath of an Almighty Creator God whose Holy anger is ever pressing down upon us harder and harder in an eternal hell from which there is no escape!

If we were to receive Mercy, we would receive no more than the spiritual blindness from which we suffer and nothing else. There would be NO Salvation, only mercy in that God has not already passed a sentence on us!

But this is where God meets us! In Grace, He reaches out to us in our condemnation and rescues us from His wrath. Grace is where God chooses to see His Son's righteousness in our place and our wretchedness in His.

It is GRACE that not only pays the price for our condemnation, but it is GRACE that adopts us as sons and daughters of the Most High!

God takes those ruined by their sin and shows them undeserved, un-coerced favor in Jesus Christ!

We become Spiritually Alive

It is God Himself who makes us spiritually alive and opens our hearts, ears, and minds to His truth and the richness of His word.

> I will sprinkle clean water on you, and you shall be clean from all your uncleanness's, and from all your idols I will cleanse you. And I will give you a new heart, and a new spirit I will put within you. And I will remove the heart of stone from your flesh and give you a heart of flesh. And I will put my Spirit within you and cause you to walk in my statutes and be careful to obey my rules.
>
> Ezekiel 36:25-27

We become Morally Empowered

We are finally able to refuse that temptation that had so beguiled us in the past, to look at that which had enslaved us before and turn away from it, to "Go and sin no more."

> We were therefore buried with him through baptism into death in order that, just as Christ was raised from the dead through the glory of the Father, we too may live a new life. For if we have been united with him in a death like his, we will certainly also be united with him in a resurrection like his. For we know that our old self was crucified with him so that the body ruled by sin might be one away with that we should no longer be slaves to sin because anyone who has died has been set free from sin.
>
> Romans 6:4-7

> By grace you have been saved and raised up with him and seated with him in the heavenly places in Christ Jesus.
>
> Ephesians 2:6

In the past, God looked at us through the lens of wrath, but now God looks at us in Jesus Christ, beautiful and glorious, already seated with Jesus in His presence! Our standing has changed from condemned to glorified. Such grace should take our breath away and cause us to sing with John Newton . . . Amazing Grace, how sweet the sound that saved a wretch like me. I once was lost but now am found, was blind but now I see!

Grace transforms everything as we learn that we are loved NOT because we have performed well or met certain standards of living, but because we are united in Christ. Empowered by this union with Jesus, we live new lives of worship and service as agents of the Kingdom to come. The reason we do not really understand God's grace is that we fail to understand our own ruin, who we are as sinners, our condition of spiritual deadness and moral captivity, and how utterly repulsive even our littlest sin is to a Holy and Righteous God!

Magnifying God

God's purpose has remained the same—that God might glorify and enjoy Himself forever as we glorify Him and enjoy Him forever!

> "Thus says the Lord God: It is not for your sake, O house of Israel, that I am about to act, but for the sake of my holy name, which you have profaned among the nations to which you came. And I will vindicate the holiness of my great name, which has been profaned among the nations, the nations will know that I am the Lord, declares the Lord God, when through you I vindicate my holiness before their eyes—It is not for your sake that I will act, declares the Lord God; let that be known to you."
>
> Ezekiel 36:22-23, 25-27, 31-33

Magnifying Christ. After all, it's by virtue of our relationship with His Son that we receive His Grace in the first place. Christ, the King, is the glorious One for whom our hearts long. And God pours out the riches of His Grace so that we might magnify God's own Son!

> And He said to him, "Truly, truly, I say to you, you will see the heavens opened and the angels of God ascending and descending on the Son of Man."
>
> John 1:51

Our Response—Gratitude

> Let not sin therefore reign in your mortal body, to make you obey its passions. Do not present your members to sin as instruments for unrighteousness but present yourselves to God as those who have been brought from death to life, and your members to God as instruments for righteousness. For sin will have no dominion over you since you are not under law but under grace.
>
> Romans 6:12-14

There can be only one proper response to grace: a life of grateful holiness.

Christians, whose sins are forgiven, should now live in holy, obedient gratitude for the grace they have received. Grateful law-keeping is the saved sinner's response to received grace. The rest of our lives are a way of saying, "Thank you."

Christians are called to a life of holiness, holiness motivated by gratitude for all that God has done for them in the gospel of Jesus Christ.

As with prayer, stroll often past the cross of Christ and gaze thoughtfully at it, remembering the reason that this was necessary, the depths of your corruption and sin, as well as the great sacrifice that was made there on your behalf.

CHAPTER 7

Faith

Camping, Sun Outdoors, Narvon, PA.

I made these reservations in March of this year. Because Scott is unable to drive due to his seizure, we arranged to have our youngest son drive the camper for us. Unfortunately, his father-in-law became quite ill during this time and was unable to drive the truck and needed to spend time with his wife. Shortly after we left to go to the campsite, Scottie noticed that something had come off the camper. Waving down the driver and pulling into a vacant parking lot, we found that the front left wheel bearing had spun off. My sons have GREAT friends. Within two hours, the bearing was replaced and repacked with grease (one of them took the hub off of his own camper to replace ours and get us back on the road). After we finally got checked in at the campground and settled in, we received a phone call from our daughter-in-law, asking if we could take care of our granddaughter for a night or two. Her dad's body was shutting down and would not last long. His greatest desire was to hold his granddaughter (so very sad). Funerals and viewings wrapped up the week and we finally had a chance to get home. I must say that the vacation was wonderful and my wife and I got to spend some GREAT time together. It sure was exhausting. Five full weeks away in six.

Lori

The Christ in my Cancer

As I commented earlier, my wonderful wife and I spent time laughing, crying, hugging each other, and talking about things we needed to talk about. For the first time since having children, we became friends all over again as we appreciated and simply "dated" each other again.

> He said to them, "Because of your little faith. For truly, I say to you, if you have faith like a grain of mustard seed, you will say to this mountain, Move from here to there and it will move, and nothing will be impossible for you.—and whatever you ask in prayer, you will receive, if you have faith."
>
> Matthew 17:20, 21:22

> So, faith comes from hearing, and hearing through the word of Christ.
>
> Romans 10:17

> And without faith it is impossible to please him, for whoever would draw near to God must believe that he exists and that he rewards those who seek him.
>
> Hebrews 11:6

> For by grace you have been saved through faith. And this is not your own doing; it is the gift of God, not a result of works, so that no one may boast. For we are his workmanship, created in Christ Jesus for good works, which God prepared beforehand, that we should walk in them.
>
> Ephesians 2:8-10

> And Jesus answered them, "Have faith in God. Truly, I say to you, whoever says to this mountain, 'Be taken up and thrown into the sea', and does not doubt in his heart, but believes that what he says will come to pass, it will

Faith

be done for him. Therefore, I tell you, whatever you ask in prayer, believe that you have received it, and it will be yours."

Mark 11:22-24

The above passages from Scripture all speak of faith, but if we read them together, they seem to tell a contradictory story—certainly a confusing one to say the least.

"If you have faith the size of a mustard seed [which is only one millimeter, by the way] you will say to this mountain, 'Move from here to there,' and it will move. Nothing will be impossible for you. Whatever you ask in prayer, you will receive if you have [enough] faith. Truly, I say to you, whoever says to this mountain, 'Be taken up and thrown into the sea,' and does not doubt in his heart, it will be done for him. Whatever you ask in prayer, believe that you have received it, and it will be yours." (It is this heretical interpretation that is at the Heart of the Prosperity Doctrine).

BUT ... Without faith it is impossible to please God, for by grace you have been saved through faith and this is not your own doing, it is the gift of God. Faith comes from hearing and hearing through the word of Christ.

How do we make sense of the multitude of Scriptures that speak to us about faith? What does it mean to have "faith the size of a mustard seed"? Can we indeed ask for ANYTHING and be assured that it will come to pass? If I believe beforehand that I will receive what I ask for in prayer will it really be given to me? How do God's providence and sovereignty play into all of this? Precisely how much faith is enough? How does doubt enter into the equation? How do doubt and faith work themselves out in the answers to prayer?

I cannot possibly please God without faith, yet Scripture tells us that this faith is a gift from God.

So, if God does not give me the gift of faith then I cannot possibly please Him? But Scripture tells us that faith comes by hearing and hearing comes from the Word of Christ—So if I listen to the Bible on audiotape once through, won't I have faith?

J.P Moreland is quoted as saying "I think that many people today, both in the church and in the world, perceive faith as believing when there is absolutely no reason to believe at all. They regard it as a blind leap in the dark or as an irrational feeling of closeness to God."

Faith is Intellectual

Faith rests not on ignorance, but on knowledge. And this is indeed knowledge not only of God but ALSO of the Divine Will.

James Boice speaks of this in his sermon The Serpent in the Wilderness: "We do not obtain salvation because we are prepared to embrace as true whatever the church has prescribed, or because we turn over to the Church, the Pastor, the Sunday School Teacher etc. the task of inquiring and knowing, but we obtain salvation when we know that God is our merciful Father, because of reconciliation effected through Christ, and that Christ has been given to us as righteousness, sanctification, and life. By this knowledge, I say, not by submission to our feelings do we obtain entry into the kingdom of heaven."[9]

Faith is Rooted in Proper Doctrine

Today we live in one of the most doctrinally ignorant times in history. If you were to ask most people about Church Doctrine you would likely get the answer that they, "aren't interested in doctrine, they just want Jesus," and they point to passages like Matthew 18:3 to defend their position "Truly, I say to you, unless you turn and become like children, you will never enter the kingdom of heaven."

Think about how ridiculous that statement is for just a second. Without proper doctrine how can you know that you are following the right Jesus? Are you worshipping the Jesus of Scripture in

---

9   Boice, J. M. (n.d.), The Serpent in the Wilderness: Alliance of Confessing Evangelicals. https://www.alliancenet.org/tab/thursday-knowledge-and-true-belief-numbers-214-9. Viewed October 11, 2022

which Jesus is a co-equal member of the Trinity consisting of God the Father, God the Son, and God the Holy Spirit? Perhaps you are following the Jesus of Islam wherein Jesus was a prophet of God and not at all God Himself? Maybe you worship the Jesus of the Druze faith who view Jesus as both Prophet AND Messiah—Yet still NOT part of the Trinity? Or the Baha'i Faith which considers Jesus to be one of the many manifestations of God—a series of personages who reflect the attributes of the divine in the human world? Possibly you follow Sikhism which views Jesus as a highly-ranked Holy man or saint. Or you may follow the Jesus of the Latter-day Saints who believe Jesus Christ is the literal son of God and as such is a distinctly unique being apart from God and therefore reduced to the status of "a" god.

Doctrine roots us in the Truth of God's Word. Knowledge of His Word keeps us from straying onto "the path that leads to destruction." Without proper doctrine, we will ultimately fall prey to the Philosophy of the Age. As Alexander Henderson puts it "An ignorant faith is no faith at all."

Yes, Jesus does indeed want us to have a child-like faith, but certainly not a childish one!

It means that we are to have a faith that is as accepting and trusting as that of a child, a faith born in innocence rather than ignorance, a faith that is maturing in wisdom, not one that remains at the intellectual level of a child!

> About this, we have much to say, and it is hard to explain, since you have become dull of hearing. For though by this time, you ought to be teachers, you need someone to teach you again the basic principles of the oracles of God. You need milk, not solid food, for everyone who lives on milk is unskilled in the word of righteousness, since he is a child. But solid food is for the mature, for those who have their powers of discernment trained by constant practice to distinguish good from evil. [Why?] so that we may no longer be children—tossed to and fro

by the waves and carried about by every wind of doctrine, by human cunning, by craftiness in deceitful schemes.

Hebrews 5:11-14, Ephesians 4:14

Proper Doctrine is Commanded by God

And these words that I command you today shall be on your heart. You shall teach them diligently to your children and shall talk of them when you sit in your house, and when you walk by the way, and when you lie down, and when you rise. You shall bind them as a sign on your hand, and they shall be as frontlets between your eyes. You shall write them on the doorposts of your house and on your gates.

Deuteronomy 6:6-9

Proper Doctrine Protects us from error

As I urged you when I was going to Macedonia, remain at Ephesus so that you may charge certain persons not to teach any different doctrine, nor to devote themselves to myths and endless genealogies, which promote speculations rather than the stewardship from God that is by faith. The aim of our charge is love that issues from a pure heart and a good conscience and a sincere faith. Certain persons, by swerving from these, have wandered away into vain discussion, desiring to be teachers of the law, without understanding either what they are saying or the things about which they make confident assertions.

1 Timothy 1:3-7

The example of studying Doctrine was demonstrated by early believers.

And they devoted themselves to the apostles' teaching and the fellowship, to the breaking of bread and the prayers.

Faith

Acts 2:42

For Jesus, Proper Doctrine was certainly not irrelevant, it was the primary means by which men and women will become His followers!

> And Jesus came and said to them, "All authority in heaven and on earth has been given to me. Go therefore and make disciples of all nations, baptizing them in the name of the Father and of the Son and of the Holy Spirit, teaching them to observe all that I have commanded you. And behold, I am with you always, to the end of the age."
>
> Mathew 28:18-20

Faith is Relational

Genuine faith must be more though than purely intellectual knowledge. Even Satan and his imps have an intellectual knowledge of God and yet they are doomed. True faith has an intellectual knowledge of God while at the same time being engaged in a relationship with Him.

Luther and Calvin both knew that true faith involved a relationship with God much like that of a husband and wife. More than an intellectual "knowing" but also an intimate relational "knowing" as well.

The Bible uses the word "knowing" in a relational manner frequently.

> On that day many will say to me, Lord, Lord, did we not prophesy in your name, and cast out demons in your name, and do many mighty works in your name? And then will I declare to them, I never knew you; depart from me, you workers of lawlessness.
>
> Matthew 7:22-33

This cannot possibly be an "intellectual" knowing since Jesus obviously knew enough to pronounce them "Workers of Lawlessness" so then this MUST be a relational "knowing"

What Jesus is saying in Matthew 7 is that He never had a relationship with them!

This word "know" tells us as well that not only is faith relational, but it is also the most intimate kind of relationship!

> When Joseph woke from sleep, he did as the angel of the Lord commanded him: he took his wife but knew her not until she had given birth to a son. And he called his name Jesus.
>
> Matthew 1:24-25

A true and saving faith not only has an intellectual understanding of God through His word, but it also has an intimate ongoing growing relationship with Jesus Christ, loving Him and clinging to Him with all our heart!

Faith is rooted in Trust

Saving faith not only involves an intellectual knowledge of God and a relationship with Him but it equally involves trusting Him.

We are to Trust Him . . .

This means 'resting' or 'leaning' on Christ in much the same way a weary pilgrim might lean on a staff or cane.

Christians are to trust in Christ and Christ Alone. Not in themselves, not in their own abilities or resources, not in the government or any other person, not even in the Church, Pastor, Sunday School Teacher, etc.!

> For you, O Lord, are my hope, my trust, O Lord, from my youth. Upon you I have leaned from before my birth; you are he who took me from my mother's womb. My praise is continually of you.
>
> Psalm 71:5-6

Faith

Trust in the (Church? Pastor? Sunday School Teacher? and Favorite Author?) with all your heart? No.

> Trust IN THE LORD with all your heart and do not lean on your own understanding. In all your ways acknowledge him, and he will make straight your paths. Be not wise in your own eyes; fear the Lord and turn away from evil. It will be healing to your flesh and refreshment to your bones.
>
> Proverbs 3:5-8

Trust is Experiential

Trust built on knowledge gained through experience and inspection . . .

What is it you trust and why do you trust it? Think about it for a moment . . .

You trust your radiologist or Oncologist to treat your Brain Cancer diagnosis, but why do you trust this Doctor over others?

You trust your car to safely deliver you to your destination and back again. Why?

You trust that the airplane you are boarding will hold together and that the pilot knows how to fly it. Why?

You trust the butcher that processes your meat, the hairdresser, the vet, the cashier, the chef, the mechanic . . .

The Diabetic trusts that the medicine in her vial is not corrupted . . .

But WHY do we trust all of these people and devices?

We trust them because our experience tells us that we can—either through a personal relationship, the experience of others we trust, or through research beforehand.

Our trust is built directly upon what we know and have experienced!

Simply put, we cannot trust God unless we have first experienced God!

Christian faith trusts Christ, not because it is a blind leap but precisely because it knows Him!

Faith expresses itself in Activity

Faith is not a work. It does nothing, offers nothing, accomplishes nothing, brings nothing, and earns nothing. Faith is a diseased hand that is capable of doing nothing except receiving that which God freely gives!

Faith IS however EXPRESSED in works. Where there is a true saving faith there are also works that glorify the one that has given that faith!

> What good is it, my brothers, if someone says he has faith but does not have works? Can that faith save him? If a brother or sister is poorly clothed and lacking in daily food, and one of you says to them, "Go in peace, be warmed and filled," without giving them the things needed for the body, what good is that? So also faith by itself, if it does not have works, is dead.
>
> James 2:14-17

Faith is not necessarily strong

> "The kingdom of heaven is like a grain of mustard seed that a man took and sowed in his field. It is the smallest of all seeds, but when it has grown it is larger than all the garden plants and becomes a tree, so that the birds of the air come and make nests in its branches."
>
> Matthew 13:31-32

How do God's providence and sovereignty play into this? Prayer is the "means" by which God Works. Where do our prayers fit into the operations of God's sovereign rule over His creation?

> Elijah was a man with a nature like ours, and he prayed fervently that it might not rain, and for three years and six months, it did not rain on the earth. Then he prayed again,

Faith

and the heaven gave rain, and the earth bore its fruit.

Is anyone among you sick? Let him call for the elders of the church, and let them pray over him, anointing him with oil in the name of the Lord. And the prayer of faith will save the one who is sick, and the Lord will raise him up. And if he has committed sins, he will be forgiven.

James 5:17-18, 14-15

God could have easily withheld the rain in Elijah's day, could have opened the skies when He was ready, heal at his own initiative apart from the prayers of others. But, God uses prayer as the catalyst to His answer and the conduit to His actions, actions by the way, that were determined from before eternity! I'll say it again, I have Brain Cancer because Jesus Christ ordained it to be so according to His will and His grace. May He receive all the glory for it in the remainder of my life and from this book.

To say that, "God waits on our prayers" recognizes the Glory of God's wisdom and His unfathomable greatness as He knits our prayers into the outworking of His eternal plan! Prayer is God's means for God's ends, intended by God to engage us in the accomplishment of His purposes for His own glory and goals! If we learn anything from this passage it is that our faith can be very small indeed and still be a genuine saving, Faith.

One theologian said that if a man falls into a river, he will probably grasp the branch of a tree to keep himself from perishing. Likewise, we weakly grasp Christ with our faith amid sins, death, and distress. However small that faith may be, it saves us. It rules over death and treads the devil underfoot.

CHAPTER 8

Discipleship

Golfing and Dinner with our son:

My dad passed away in the spring of 2021 and he loved to golf. So much so, he taught my second son to golf as well. I have always liked golfing, but seldom get a chance to play very often. About a week before we went on our trips, I had a chance to play 9 holes with my son and had a wonderful time with him. We seldom see eye to eye on much, but I love him dearly and it would seem he loves me just as much. This weekend we are going to get a bunch of wiffle golf balls and bang them around the yard while grilling some beef and plumb kabobs and some chicken and apricot kabobs too. Very excited. This was the son that told us about the Week Away Foundation that provided the trip to Ocean City. So glad he brought it to our attention and that I was not too proud to accept it. We were truly blessed by these "times away".

God provided perfect weather nearly every day with light breezes and beautiful sunshine. We did have a bit of rough weather as we drove to and from at night but it rarely lasted or posed a problem for us as we drove to and from.

Lori

All People must at some point in their existence stand in the presence of God and be judged. There are only two possible outcomes—either guilt or innocence, condemnation or justification which demands absolute perfect righteousness.

"Sola Gratia" (by Grace Alone)
„Sola Christus" (In Christ Alone)
"Sola Fide" (Through Faith Alone)

> Then God said, "Let us make man in our image, after our likeness... And it was so. And God saw everything that he had made, and behold, it was very good."
>
> Genesis 1:26a, 31a

> And the Lord God commanded the man, saying, "You may surely eat of every tree of the garden, but of the tree of the knowledge of good and evil you shall not eat, for in the day that you eat of it you shall surely die."
>
> Genesis 2:16-17

> Now the serpent was more crafty than any other beast of the field that the Lord God had made... when the woman saw that the tree was good for food, and that it was a delight to the eyes, and that the tree was to be desired to make one wise, she took of its fruit and ate, and she also gave some to her husband who was with her, and he ate. Then the eyes of both were opened, and they knew that they were naked. And they sewed fig leaves together and made themselves loincloths.
>
> Genesis 3:1, 6-7

> Then the Lord God said to the serpent, "I will put enmity between you and the woman, and between your offspring and her offspring; he shall bruise your head, and you shall bruise his heel."
>
> Genesis 3:15

> What then shall we say was gained by Abraham, our forefather according to the flesh? For if Abraham was justified by works, he has something to boast about, but

Discipleship

not before God. For what does the Scripture say? Abraham believed God, and it was counted to him as righteousness.

Romans 4:1-3

PART 2

The Armor of God

Part 2 is here because once we have that proper faith relationship with Jesus Christ, the enemy of our souls will attack us at every front, and we need to understand how to defend ourselves in the fight that will inevitably come our way. Nearly all of us have at some point "Put on the Whole Armor of God" which sounds great, but how do we do that exactly? Part 2 is written to give us the skills and knowledge in the use of the armor and the purposes of each piece as we "put it on."

CHAPTER 9

A Call to Arms

D. Martyn Lloyd-Jones; "The Christian Soldier—The Call to Battle" states, "There is nothing that is more urgently important for all who claim the name of Christian, than to grasp and to understand the teaching of this section of Scripture. I say those who claim the name of Christian, because the Apostle's words are obviously addressed to Christian people and to Christian people only. They have no message for those who are not Christians; indeed, nobody else can understand them. The world today ridicules this kind of statement. It does not believe in a spiritual realm at all. It is even doubtful about the being of God; it has no faith in the Lord Jesus Christ; still less, therefore, does it believe that there are principalities and powers, the rulers of the darkness of this world, spiritual wickedness even in high (or in heavenly) places. Such words are meaningless to the world; it has no appreciation of their value and importance. But to the Christian the statement is not only full of significance, it is also full of help and of real encouragement; and, let me repeat, there is surely no theme that is more urgently important to all Christians at the present time than just this. I refer, of course, to the whole state of life, the whole state of the world, and to all the difficulty of living, and especially living the Christian life in these confused times in which we find ourselves. Not that I suggest that life has ever been easy in this world for the Christian. It was not so for the early Christians. And today, in some respects, the problem is more acute and more urgent, perhaps, than it has ever been. There was a time, until comparatively recently, when at least a man's home was shut off from the world; but now the world comes into the home in many ways, not only with the newspapers but with the television and the wireless and other media. Thus, the fight of faith becomes particularly difficult and strenuous for the Christian at such a time; and in addition to all this there is the general strain of the times and anxiety of the hour."[10]

> Finally, be strong in the Lord and in the strength of his might. Put on the whole armor of God, so that you may be able to stand against the schemes of the devil. For we do not wrestle against flesh and blood, but against the rulers, against the authorities, against the cosmic powers over this present darkness, against the spiritual forces of evil in the heavenly places. Therefore, take up the whole armor of God, that you may be able to withstand in the evil day, and having done all, to stand firm. Stand therefore, having fastened on the belt of truth, and having put on the breastplate of righteousness, and, as shoes for your feet, having put on the readiness given by the gospel of peace. In all circumstances take up the shield of faith, with which you can extinguish all the flaming darts of the evil one; and take the helmet of salvation, and the sword of the Spirit, which is the word of God, praying at all times in the Spirit, with all prayer and supplication. To that end keep alert with all perseverance, making supplication for all the saints, and also for me, that words may be given to me in opening my mouth boldly to proclaim the mystery of the gospel.
>
> Ephesians 6:10-19

---

[10] Lloyd-Jones, M. (n.d.), The Call to Battle - A Sermon from Dr. Martyn Lloyd Jones. https://www.mljtrust.org/sermons-online/ephesians-6-10-13/the-call-to-battle/. Viewed October 11, 2022

A Call to Arms

Note From our text in Ephesians 6 the intensity of the commands given and the reasons for them!

"The Lord is a man of war; Jehovah is His name" (Exodus 15:3)

"Put On" the whole armor of God

The whole armor—not part of it. This is not to be a halfhearted effort on our part. That it is the very first command regarding the armor in this passage we can infer that this is a matter of the highest priority and indicates that we are defenseless and feckless in this war without first covering our vital organs with the full implementation of God's armor.

It is a command, not a request, and requires action on our part.

Notice also that there is no provision in this passage for removing the armor once it is put on. We are told to "Put On the Whole Armor of God" and it is to remain on us for the remainder of our lives. Can you guess then how long this war will wage?

Stand against the Schemes of the Devil

Have you noticed that there is absolutely no armor for the back! What this means is that we are given orders that do not include retreat! Stand in this passage means that we are to be resolved, committed, fully armored—sword in hand and ready to give battle so that when the Devil comes at you with his schemes you are prepared to ward them off and defeat the attack. This passage also tells us that the Devil WILL INDEED come after us with all the same deceptive wiles and lies that have cost so many millions their souls since man fell in Eden. Make no mistake that unless we get this passage of scripture right, we too, every one of us, are susceptible to falling into this battle and succumbing to the "Schemes of the Devil".

> Now the Spirit expressly says that in later times some will depart from the faith by devoting themselves to deceitful spirits and teachings of demons.
>
> 1 Timothy 4:1

The Christ in my Cancer

We "Wrestle" against . . . Note here that we are to "wrestle". It is a word that indicates actual, positive, definite contact with our foe. We must also understand who our enemy is to do battle with and gain victory over him.

Our enemy IS NOT Flesh and Blood.

Our enemy is not our neighbor, it is not the President or congress, republicans or the democrats. Our enemy is not another nation or religion, ISIS or Al Qaida.

Our enemy is not heart disease or cancer or diabetes. It is not old age or Alzheimer's.

In truth, our enemy is our own father, the devil. Unless we are delivered from our sins by the life death and resurrection of Jesus Christ it is our own father who deceives us and drags us with him into Hell.

> "You are of your father the devil, and your will is to do your father's desires. He was a murderer from the beginning, and does not stand in the truth, because there is no truth in him. When he lies, he speaks out of his own character, for he is a liar and the father of lies."
>
> John 8:44

Our enemy IS the rulers and authorities and cosmic powers over this present age -the spiritual forces of evil in the heavenly places. In God the Father, there is essential government. In the "god of this world," there is disorder and evil. In God the Son, there is grace and forgiveness. In Satan, there is condemnation and damnation. In God the Holy Spirit, there is guidance and truth. In the Devil, there is deception and falsehood.

Our enemy, as described in Scripture is an anointed cherub and the Prince of Demons.

> You were an anointed guardian cherub. I placed you; you were on the holy mountain of God; in the midst of the stones of fire you walked.
>
> Ezekiel 28:14

A Call to Arms

> But some of them said, He casts out demons by Beelzebul, the prince of demons,
>
> Luke 11:15

The god of this world.
The prince of the power of the air.

> in which you once walked, following the course of this world, following the prince of the power of the air, the spirit that is now at work in the sons of disobedience
>
> Ephesians 2:2

> In their case the god of this world has blinded the minds of the unbelievers, to keep them from seeing the light of the gospel of the glory of Christ, who is the image of God.
>
> 2 Corinthians 4:4

Our enemy is actively involved in opposing God's work.

> Then he showed me Joshua the high priest standing before the angel of the LORD, and Satan standing at his right hand to accuse him. All while perverting God's Word.
>
> Zechariah 3:1

> and said to him, "If you are the Son of God, throw yourself down, for it is written, 'He will command his angels concerning you,' and 'On their hands they will bear you up, lest you strike your foot against a stone.'"
>
> Matthew 4:6

Hindering God's servants (that would be us).

> Wherefore we would have come unto you, even I Paul, once and again; but Satan hindered us.

He Hinders the Gospel.

1 Thessalonians 2:18

> In whom the god of this world hath blinded the minds of them which believe not, lest the light of the glorious gospel of Christ, who is the image of God, should shine unto them.
>
> He ensnares the Righteous.
>
> 2 Corinthians 4:4
>
> Moreover, he must have a good report of them which are without; lest he fall into reproach and the snare of the devil.
>
> 1 Timothy 3:7
>
> He holds this world in his power. And we know that we are of God, and the whole world lieth in wickedness.
>
> 1 John 5:19

This is a terrible fact that we must all face. We wrestle. Our enemy patiently waits for our moment of weakness and then strikes with sudden mercilessness and "pins us to the mat". There is much to be understood of the enemies' tactics when we examine the word "considered" in Job chapter 1 when God asks Satan if he has, "considered my servant Job?"

Satan is watching and waiting for a moment of weakness and the most effective place to strike. A home is only as secure as its least guarded door and the Devil is waiting for that moment when your attention is distracted away from that particular door and when you are unaware, he breaks in and begins his assault.

There are those whom he will never tempt with alcohol because for them alcohol is no temptation. Your weakest point is where he will attack whether it is pride, passion, lust, intellectuality, emotional weakness, etc.

Take Up the Whole Armor of God

Notice the difference in this passage from verse 1 which tells us to "Put On" the whole armor of God. Here we are told to "Take Up" the whole armor of God.

Is Paul getting a bit senile in his old age? Maybe didn't get enough sleep the night before, he is repeating himself? Now understand that in Scripture, authors typically repeat words to indicate emphasis but that doesn't seem to work here, so either Paul really is repeating himself or the term "Take Up" holds a different meaning from "Put On".

In this case "Take Up" means that we are not to display the armor, or to carry it around in a backpack until we think we may need it. The intent here is that we are already on the battlefield and need to already be prepared for battle. This passage is telling us that we are to actively "wield" the weapons and armor that God has provided for us. We are not to be idle, simply standing on the sidelines waiting for Satan to come our way and attack us.

You are standing at this very moment on the battlefield, facing your deadliest enemy. He will not rest until he has captured your soul and condemned it with his to the eternal torment of Hell! If you are not fully prepared to do battle with him you will not survive.

Withstand in the evil day

We have no orders from our Commander in Chief to negotiate a truce and get the best "terms" of surrender possible. We are not to cease from conflict and try to be as agreeable as we can with our Lord's foes. No such orders are given here. We are to secure the armor, grab our sword and go forth to fight the enemies of our Lord.

We have no orders to be quiet or "sit this one out". We are to "take the sword". If we properly understand God's will in this we will eventually get to heaven with His sword in hand, we will be bloodied and bruised, gasping with exhaustion from our efforts. We will have battled our way right up to the gates of heaven for His sake!

Stand Firm

Submit to God and resist. There is a profound reason for this. The root cause of the whole matter of armor and warfare comes down to one simple thing—pride and rebellion. Satan's sin was a rebellion against God and his plan is to keep us in rebellion from God as well! It is only in submission to God that we can effectively "stand firm" as we are here commanded.

In fact, James tells us the primary issues in this conflict and God's actions against it. It is pride and God directly and actively opposes it!

> God opposes the proud but gives grace to the humble. Submit yourselves therefore to God. Resist the devil, and he will flee from you. Draw near to God, and he will draw near to you. Cleanse your hands, you sinners, and purify your hearts, you double-minded.
>
> James 4:6b-8

The other part of this passage that goes "hand in hand" with submission is resistance. Both our submission to God and our resistance to the devil are necessary for us to be victorious in battle. In Hebrews, we also see an indication of conditions on this battlefield!

> Consider him who endured from sinners such hostility against himself, so that you may not grow weary or fainthearted. In your struggle against sin you have not yet resisted to the point of shedding your blood.
>
> Hebrews 12:3-4

Stand, Therefore

This is the third "Stand" in this passage. Remember what I said about repetition being used to provide emphasis? I believe that this is what we see here with the 3 "Stand". If that is the case, then we should get a grasp of the immediate and urgent call that we "Stand" against the devil.

A Call to Arms

"Therefore," calls us to look back at the previous statements regarding the warfare that we invariably find ourselves in, and in understanding this we must finally "Stand." There is no retreat, no surrender, and no negotiations that bring peace. We are "all in" in this war and as a result, our commitment to stand must never waiver!

"Fastened" on the Belt of Truth, "Put On" the Breastplate of Righteousness, "Put On" the Readiness of the Gospel of Peace, "Take Up" the Shield of Faith, "Extinguish" "All The Flaming Darts" of the evil one

Our adversary is subtle in his methods. Scripture describes him as an "angel of light", a "roaring lion", the "prince of this world". These descriptions are not to be taken literally because they do not imply physical appearance but the tactics by which our enemy attacks.

He wields each of his weapons as the occasion and purpose of his attack require. To deceive and confuse "even the elect," he appears as an "angel of light," confusing and confounding with words that sound right, feel right and make sense. These words of his, though, are designed to lead us timidly (as lambs to the slaughter) to our own destruction.

> "And then many will fall away and betray one another and hate one another. And many false prophets will arise and lead many astray. And because lawlessness will be increased, the love of many will grow cold."
>
> Matthew 24:12

> For such men are false apostles, deceitful workmen, disguising themselves as apostles of Christ. And no wonder, for even Satan disguises himself as an angel of light. So it is no surprise if his servants, also, disguise themselves as servants of righteousness. Their end will correspond to their deeds.
>
> 2 Corinthians 11:13-15

The Christ in my Cancer

He comes as would a roaring lion, intimidating with awful ferocity and fierceness that he might overwhelm the timid and afraid.

> "Be sober-minded; be watchful. Your adversary the devil prowls around like a roaring lion, seeking someone to devour. Resist him, firm in your faith, knowing that the same kinds of suffering are being experienced by your brotherhood throughout the world."
> 1 Peter 5:8-9

As the prince of the world, he offers to us all the kingdoms and riches the world has to offer, looking to entrap us, spoil us, and damn us as he demands our homage to him in return.

> "Now is the judgment of this world; now will the ruler of this world be cast out"

> "Take" the Helmet of Salvation AND The Sword of the Spirit, "Praying at all Times" in the Spirit, "Keep Alert With All Perseverance."
> John 12:31

Like the "watchman on the hill," we are to be constantly vigilant because our enemy is extremely patient and is willing to wait and hide as long as it takes for us to lower our guard. As a result of a lack of vigilance, the enemy has now infiltrated himself into half of our theology, most of our church pulpits, and almost every single one of our newfangled church philosophies and theatrics.

There is an enormous responsibility as well with our command to be vigilant.

> Son of man, I have made you a watchman for the house of Israel. Whenever you hear a word from my mouth, you shall give them warning from me. If I say to the wicked, 'You shall surely die,' and you give him no warning, nor

A Call to Arms

speak to warn the wicked from his wicked way, in order to save his life, that wicked person shall die for his iniquity, but his blood I will require at your hand. But if you warn the wicked, and he does not turn from his wickedness, or from his wicked way, he shall die for his iniquity, but you will have delivered your soul.

Ezekiel 3:17-19

"Making Supplication" for all the saints

We need to understand that we are not called to a life of ease and luxury, but to a life on the battlefield. A lifetime of warfare of the absolute highest intensity!

so that through the church the manifold wisdom of God might now be made known to the rulers and authorities in the heavenly places.

Ephesians 3:10

This charge I entrust to you, Timothy, my child, in accordance with the prophecies previously made about you, that by them you may wage the good warfare, holding faith and a good conscience. By rejecting this, some have made shipwreck of their faith, among whom are Hymenaeus and Alexander, whom I have handed over to Satan that they may learn not to blaspheme.

1 Timothy 1:18

Note here that in rejecting the Gospel, and thereby committing blasphemy, we may be handed over to the commanding general of the enemy!

Do not be overcome by evil but overcome evil with good.

Romans 12:21

> For you are all children of light, children of the day. We are not of the night
>
> or of the darkness. So then let us not sleep, as others do, but let us keep awake and be sober.
>
> 1 Thessalonians 5:5-6

> "I will build my church, and the gates of hell shall not prevail against it."
>
> Matthew 16:18

> Fight the good fight of the faith . . .
>
> 1 Timothy 6:12a

There is absolutely no middle ground in this war. No neutral parties, nobody "sitting it out". You are either on the side of Jesus Christ in this war or you are fighting actively for Satan—period!

> "Whoever is not with me is against me, and whoever does not gather with me scatters."
>
> Matthew 12:30

Note again that there is no provision in this armor whatsoever for retreat! Any retreat would result in leaving our backs completely exposed to the enemy's "Flaming Darts"!

The armor consists of: The Belt of Truth, The Breastplate of Righteousness, Shoes as the Readiness of the Gospel of Peace, The Shield of Faith, The Helmet of Salvation, and The Sword of the Spirit

You stand in the Name of the Lord wherever you are, as a point of resistance to the enemy of righteousness. You don't stand alone, however. You are but one of a grand multitude, that great army of people whom the Lord has ransomed for His own, by His own blood, and for His own purpose!

> For though we walk in the flesh, we are not waging war according to the flesh. For the weapons of our warfare

A Call to Arms

are not of the flesh but have divine power to destroy strongholds. We destroy arguments and every lofty opinion raised against the knowledge of God and take every thought captive to obey Christ, being ready to punish every disobedience, when your obedience is complete.

> 2 Corinthians 10:3-6

Life is hard—especially for those of us who follow Jesus Christ. Our own Savior warns us that it will be so. The world and its system will come after us, try to kill us, and make us ineffective on the battlefield.

Stop trying to make friends with the world, its systems, and its inhabitants! You are of a heavenly citizenry!

> And you will be hated by all for my name's sake. But the one who endures to the end will be saved.
>
> Mark 13:13

> Brother will deliver brother over to death, and the father his child, and children will rise against parents and have them put to death, and you will be hated by all for my name's sake.
>
> Matthew 10:21-22

Jesus does not paint us a very pretty picture. This is not what would be described by any rational person as our "best life now". In fact, those very teachings are mentioned by Jesus.

> "Then they will deliver you up to tribulation and put you to death, and you will be hated by all nations for my name's sake. And then many will fall away and betray one another and hate one another. And many false prophets will arise and lead many astray. And because lawlessness will be increased, the love of many will grow cold."

The Christ in my Cancer

Matthew 24:9

We are however in VERY good company. This is our comfort in times of trials and tribulations.

> "If the world hates you, know that it has hated me before it hated you. If you were of the world, the world would love you as its own; but because you are not of the world, but I chose you out of the world, therefore the world hates you. Remember the word that I said to you: 'A servant is not greater than his master.' If they persecuted me, they will also persecute you. If they kept my word, they would also keep yours. But all these things they will do to you on account of my name because they do not know him who sent me. If I had not come and spoken to them, they would not have been guilty of sin, but now they have no excuse for their sin. Whoever hates me hates my Father also. If I had not done among them the works that no one else did, they would not be guilty of sin, but now they have seen and hated both me and my Father."

John 15:18-27

Are you struggling this morning? Put on the whole armor of God! Engaged in a battle with the enemy of God? Wield the Sword of the Spirit. You see, we are each engaged in a spiritual battle every moment of our lives, and the only place from where we can effectively wage that war with the enemy of our souls is to fight him on the battlefield of Scripture!

CHAPTER 10

How Big is Your God?

Our Passion

> Whoever loves father or mother more than me is not worthy of me, and whoever loves son or daughter more than me is not worthy of me. And whoever does not take his cross and follow me is not worthy of me. Whoever finds his life will lose it, and whoever loses his life for my sake will find it.
>
> Matthew 10:37-39

Our Lives

> Only let your manner of life be worthy of the gospel of Christ, so that whether I come and see you or am absent, I may hear of you that you are standing firm in one spirit, with one mind striving side by side for the faith of the gospel, and not frightened in anything by your opponents. This is a clear sign to them of their destruction, but of your salvation, and that from God. For it has been granted to you that for the sake of Christ you should not only believe in him but also suffer for his sake, engaged in the same conflict that you saw I had and now hear that I still have.
>
> Philippians 1:27-30

The Christ in my Cancer

Our Purpose & Our Expectations

> Before I formed you in the womb I knew you, and before you were born, I consecrated you; I appointed you a prophet to the nations.
>
> Jeremiah 1:5

> Therefore, I endure everything for the sake of the elect, that they also may obtain the salvation that is in Christ Jesus with eternal glory.
>
> 2 Timothy 2:10

DC Talk said it clearly in *Jesus Freaks, vol. II*, "From the beginning of His public ministry, Jesus set the record straight: "I have Come to Change the World". He had come to change people's thinking. He had come to revolutionize their paradigm. The way they saw the world and had comfortably settled into that lifestyle, following their own desires, ignoring those around them who needed help, and figuring that was the way to do it because everyone else was doing pretty much the same thing."[11]

But then—Jesus said—"You Have Heard it Said . . . But I Say Unto You."

He came to change the world. How can those who truly follow Him have any less of a goal in life?

March 15th, 1989

My wife and I celebrated the birth of our 2nd son. We were overjoyed. Life was good for us that day. Our little family was growing and every indication at the time was that both of our children were healthy and happy. Work was going well, and as a family, we loved each other greatly. It was truly a day of celebration. Lori would spend the first few

---

11 DC Talk, Jesus Freaks, vol. II: Stories of Revolutionaries Who Changed Their World: Fearing God, Not Man: Bethany House. 2002

How Big is Your God?

days of Alec's life with him in the hospital and I returned to work and the daily routine of life. All was good—until the phone rang...

It was my wife, and she was in tears. She informed me that the doctors had found some complications with Alec's heart and that I should return to the hospital as soon as possible. Our world had just been turned upside down.

Alec had been diagnosed with several heart-related birth defects, each of which was potentially life-threatening, and he would need surgery if he was to survive. The doctors in Tampa, where we lived at the time, had done their best for him in the first 6 months or so of his life, but the problems he faced were greater than the local surgeon's skills to correct, and it was recommended that we transfer his care to the Children's Hospital of Philadelphia.

Interesting side note—I had put in an application to work for the Trane Company in King of Prussia nearly a year prior. Shortly after we were told of the need to relocate, I got a phone call from the manager of the controls group in King of Prussia asking if I would be willing to fly to Philadelphia for an interview. Needless to say, I got and took the job.

So, we moved from our home in Tampa and started over again in eastern PA, and Alec's care was transferred to CHOP. Within a week of relocating, we began to meet with the pediatric heart team at CHOP. One of the first meetings we had was with the chief of pediatric heart surgery at CHOP who informed us that if Alec was to survive, he would need extensive work to his heart and that the likelihood of his needing a heart transplant was very great and boom—just that fast, our world was once again turned upside down.

Over the past 27 years, my wife and I have put our son onto an operating room gurney and said our potential "goodbyes" to him at least a dozen times as he was wheeled away through those swinging double doors that I doubt either Lori or I will forget. To date, Alec has had more than 6 open heart surgeries in which he has had every major type of reconstruction done to his heart imaginable, several dozen cardiac catheterizations, stints installed to keep his arteries from collapsing, cadaver valves installed to replace his weakening ones, and is now under care at the University of Pennsylvania in Philadelphia for clinical heart failure—a condition for which he will eventually need the heart transplant first mentioned 27 years ago.

November 4th, 2009:

It was a day, unlike most others. Little did we know when we woke up that morning that it would be another of those days that would change the course of our lives forever.

I was at work, almost done for the day, but had one more task to complete. It meant that I had to go onto the roof of the 5-story building and diagnose an operational issue with one of the large pieces of HVAC equipment. I never did make it to the roof that day or any day since.

Installed in the building, leading from an upper-floor janitor closet to the roof, was a vertical ladder permanently mounted to the building. I had been up this very same ladder numerous times over the past year or so in the course of my work, so there was nothing unusual about it—until this day. The maintenance staff had made some repairs to this ladder system and had not done them correctly. As a result, when I reached the upper rungs of the ladder, I lost my grip and fell 10 feet or so to the bottom. I got to the first of two hospitals that day thinking that they would simply put a cast on my leg and send me home. Such was not to be the case though, as I was told that it would be at least a year until I could walk again—if I would ever be able to walk again at all. It was questionable at the time if I would even be able to keep my leg as the x-rays had shown that there were at least 32 pieces of broken bone in my lower left leg.

I spent Thanksgiving that year in a hospital bed alone for most of the day. Lori had the family to attend to for Thanksgiving, but of course, did come to sit by my bedside that evening. In the end, it took 3 different surgeries, 4 steel plates, 32 screws, and well over a year of recovery time before I could even put weight back on my leg. During that year I was confined to bed for a great portion of it, having to urinate into a milk jug since I could not get myself to the bathroom. My dear wife would come home from work each day and empty my "milk" jugs and make sure that I had food to eat.

How Big is Your God?

The other issue was work, the business, our home, and bills, not to mention the mortgage we carried as well. I should mention that being self-employed at the time of my accident left us without medical insurance and we were looking at being responsible for covering all of my medical expenses which were rapidly exceeding the one-million-dollar Mark.

In the end, I still have my leg, though I will never run again, I will never again walk normally or without pain, and the medication needed to quiet the chronic pain takes its toll on me both physically and emotionally.

August 1st, 2016:

My youngest son Aaron and his soon-to-be wife were having a baby, and since Megan is diabetic, the doctors wanted her and their baby to be checked out thoroughly to identify any potential issues for Megan or the baby. We had already been informed that my grandson would have "clubbed" feet that would need surgery to correct and that there was a possibility of some swelling in the brain, so we went with the expectation that not all was perfect, but none of us were prepared for what we were told that day.

As we sat once again in a conference room at Children's Hospital, the memories of the past 27 years all came flooding back at once and pushed themselves to the forefront of Lori's and my minds. As we listened to the doctor lay out the results of the day-long testing, it became very apparent that this would be anything but a normal pregnancy, anything but a normal child, anything but a normal life.

Colton Emerson Davis would come into this world with his very own set of challenges and the family would yet again need to adapt to a world that had once again been turned upside down.

Now, God is indeed sovereign—we all know that. And God can do anything he wishes, including the miraculous healing of Colton. But we must also face the fact that unless God decided in His wisdom to change things, Colton would very likely be born with an extreme set of challenges ranging from mental development to physical development.

The Christ in my Cancer

We were told that it was possible that Colton may never be able to walk under his own power, that he may never be able to speak or eat on his own, and that he may not even have control over his own bowels. Yes, our worlds had once again been upended. There had been many tears shed that week, tears of anguish, tears of pain, but also tears of great joy!

I experienced some of the lowest lows of my entire life that week, but thanks to the marvelous and unending grace of God I experienced some of the highest highs of my entire life as well that week.

When my future daughter-in-law posted the results of the day on Facebook, she began with "Above all else God has a plan . . ." My son responded with, "Dad, you have always taught that God is sovereign in all things. He is God and I am not. If God wants my son to be orange, then he will be orange and there is nothing I can do about it. Moreover, just because I don't understand why God made my son orange, it doesn't make his being orange any less wonderful."

Yes, life would be difficult and challenging from here on out, but as a family, we know that God is indeed in control and His perfect will shall be accomplished. None of us knows what God has planned for the future at this point, but together we are certain of several things: God is in control, God's will is perfect and ours is not, God has a plan for this that will glorify Him and sanctify us, God is always so very good—in all things. In all that lies ahead, we will praise God for the work of His hand. I am no super faithful follower, life hurts sometimes so badly that I find it impossible to hold on.

It is at these times that I recognize that it is not me that is holding onto Him, but it is He is holding onto me. No matter how Colton Emerson Davis entered this life when he entered into the life that is forever, he will do so in a way that is perfect in every respect. And finally, I have this—while it is possible in this life that I will never be able to play catch with my grandson or watch him pitch his first baseball game, I may not be able to take long walks with him and have meaningful conversations with him—I can always rest assured in the knowledge that all of these things will be restored in the next life and I will be able to walk with him and talk with him, know him and love him in a way that I can only now imagine!

One hundred short days after Colton was born, he went to be with the Lord as he pulled out his own breathing tube and breathed his last in his daddy's arms. Man, that still hurts, but as hard as it was, I can promise that little family of three had the most amazing impact for Christ that I may have ever seen as my son and his wife are two of the strongest people I have ever met. Three of Colton's nurses came to his funeral and his surgeon wanted to come but had an emergency that morning. What a testament to their faith.

February 23rd, 2022: Following a Grand Mal Seizure at work, I was Life-Flighted to the University of Pittsburgh Medical Center in Downtown Pittsburgh, where I was placed into a medically induced coma and diagnosed with three Glioblastoma tumors in my brain (an incurable form of brain cancer).

Brain surgery removed the largest from my frontal lobe and the remaining two are currently being treated with Chemotherapy and radiation. I am told that the best I can hope for is remission, but cancer will eventually return and take my life. The expectation is that I likely have 6 to 18 months to live, but in truth, I will survive exactly as long as Christ decides I will.

So, I ask again, how big is your God

How big is your God? Is He indeed sovereign in every single aspect of your life or is He only sovereign in the things that bring you joy and pleasure?

Can your God make mistakes? If God is truly Sovereign over all His creation and God is perfect in every way, then has He not directed the events of our lives, and are they not, regardless of our opinion, according to the perfect will of God?

Where are your affections? Are they living a life free of pain, struggle, and suffering?

When you pray for the pain to stop . . .

Do you consider the work that the author of that pain is doing through it?

Do you consider that what God has to give you in this struggle is far greater than what you lose through it?

Do you pray that "God's will" would be accomplished above your own desires to have the difficulty lifted from you?

Remember that Jesus Christ prayed, "Not my will but yours be done," long before we ever had to!

Do you remember that not only is God sovereign in your trials, but that He is also good, and He is loving you in them as well?

Do you consider that even this will work together for the good of God's glory?

Do you remember that all things come from the Lord? That He not only gives but also takes away, and both are to His pleasure and His Glory!

Do you remember that when He was told of Lazarus' death that Jesus wept? I believe that He wept over the pain of loss and the pain of original sin that ultimately led to the death of His friend. We should take great comfort in the fact that Jesus weeps not only for us but also weeps with us.

Applying the armor

> Three times I pleaded with the Lord about this, that it should leave me. But he said to me, "My grace is sufficient for you, for my power is made perfect in weakness." Therefore, I will boast even more gladly of my weaknesses, so that the power of Christ may rest upon me. For the sake of Christ, then, I am content with weaknesses, insults, hardships, persecutions, and calamities. For when I am weak, then I am strong.
>
> 2 Corinthians 12:8-9
> (Suffering for the sake of Christ)

Most times God sanctifies us by kicking the stuffing out of us. Hardship brings us both to God AND to the end of ourselves, just as

How Big is Your God?

Moses came to the end of himself in the heat of the desert where God molded him into the object of His will with Pharoah.
BECAUSE HE LOVES US!

> And after you have suffered a little while, the God of all grace, who has called you to his eternal glory in Christ, will himself restore, confirm, strengthen, and establish you.
>
> 1 Peter 5:10
> (Suffering is only temporary)

> ... through many tribulations we must enter the kingdom of God.
>
> Acts 14:21b
> (Suffering is essential to sanctification)

> The Lord is near to the brokenhearted and saves the crushed in spirit. Many are the afflictions of the righteous, but the Lord delivers him out of them all.
>
> Psalm 34:18-19
> (God is never far from those who suffer)

> Before I was afflicted, I went astray, but now I keep your word.
>
> It is good for me that I was afflicted, that I might learn your statutes.
>
> Psalm 119:67 & 71
> (Sanctification is often through suffering)

Jesus is not just looking for people to save—He is looking for people to follow Him Especially if it means that they must follow Him to their own death!
So, in the end, how we respond to the suffering that God brings into our lives reflects the Christ that is in our lives.

In our response to our struggles, trials, tribulations, and suffering we are, above all, to please Christ!

> No soldier gets entangled in civilian pursuits, since his aim is to please the one who enlisted him.
>
> 2 Timothy 2:4

Our response to all the difficulties of life boils down to one thing. It is the heart of the matter!

Does the world around us see in these struggles the Love of Christ? His strength? His courage in the face of defeat?

> For this very purpose I have raised you up, that I might show my power in you, and that my name might be proclaimed in all the earth.
>
> Romans 9:17
> (Insert your struggle here)

I want to leave you with one last question to think about. This is the takeaway...

What if everyone watching, reading, and listening stopped praying for God to intercede on their behalf to remove the pain in their lives and instead simply began to pray for God to "do whatever He pleases with our lives regardless of the cost to us"—and meant it!

Surrender

September 25, 2009:

God seems to be speaking in themes these days. Several conversations with friends seem to all end at the same place—Surrender. I am being convicted.

I will do my feeble best to lay out on the following pages what God has put on my heart. While I believe that God is calling me to fall on my knees and continue to leave it all at the Cross, I do not believe that this message is specifically directed toward me but to His body of believers around the world.

How Big is Your God?

I wonder how many other believers are hearing the same command today.

Jesus tells us in Matthew 20:25-28 " ... You know that the rulers of the Gentiles lord it over them, and those who are great exercise authority over them. Yet it shall not be so among you; but whoever desires to be great among you, let him be your servant and whoever desires to be first among you let him be your slave—just as the Son of Man did not come to be served but to serve, and to give His life a ransom for many."

It is important to understand one basic concept in this. We were created FOR God. He knew us before we were conceived, and He has developed a unique plan for each one of our lives. The fulfillment of that purpose is dependent on our ability to allow God to work in our lives; transforming us into Godly men and women who earnestly seek His will. God is a gentleman. He has given each of us free will in determining the direction we walk. We can choose to walk a path of our own making (which ultimately leads to despair and death) or we can choose instead to walk the path which God has laid before us. He will coax and convict us, but the decision must be ours. God will only use us; talk to us; work in us when we make the choice to place His desires above our own.

It's about a willing heart. When we make the decision to surrender to God's authority in our lives (remember we were created for His pleasure), He begins the process of transforming our hearts. He softens them and breaks them to prepare us for the work which He has planned for us. We become His apprentices in the work of His holy hand. Our priorities begin to change. We soon realize that this life is temporary, that the things which we had sought after are empty and devoid of joy. We begin to see the "Big Picture" rather than our own distorted vision of our lives.

1 Samuel 16:7 Speaks to this: "Do not look at his appearance, or at his physical stature. For the Lord does not see as man sees; for man looks at the outward appearance, but the Lord looks at the heart."

What do we see in our brothers, sisters, and friends? Do we look at the job they hold, the house they live in, and the apparent success that they enjoy, or do we see their hearts? Without surrendering to God's will in our lives we will never be able to see into the hearts of those whom we encounter every day. Without surrender, we are unable to provide the comfort and ministry which God desires of us.

In short, God wants our hearts to be His, and if we allow Him to, He will "Give them a heart to know Me, that I am the Lord; and they shall be my people and I shall be their God; for they shall return to Me with their WHOLE HEART".

God tells us in Jeremiah 24:7 that He desires our whole heart, not just a portion. In Ezekiel 18:31 He tells us to "Cast away from you all transgressions which you have committed and get yourselves a new heart and a new spirit". Here God clearly tells us that an unrepentant heart is to be cast away from us and that we should seek a new heart. That new heart can only come from the Holy Spirit, and only when we surrender to Him and allow Him to speak to it and mold it.

The question I pose to you (and myself) is this:

Will we submit all that we are body, mind, and spirit to God's will for our lives? Are we ready to give up everything to seek His face? It means that we must leave our pride behind us and walk humbly before man so that His glory will shine for all to see. It means that we must stop seeking earthly rewards and seek instead the rewards that only God can provide. It means that we must be willing to give up everything we have—wealth, home, prosperity, family, respect, and even friends at times. It means that we must walk a lonely road because it is a road that most choose to ignore or can't see. It means coming to an understanding that God's purpose can only be fulfilled in obedience. We may not know the specific purpose for which God has created us yet, but as we strive to become closer to Him, and can leave the shackles of a worldly life fall away, He will reveal to us the reason He has created each of us.

Through the turmoil of recent months, I have realized at least part of the purpose for which He saved me from death in Pittsburgh. I am no longer to seek out a pulpit—that is NOT where I am to serve Him. I have found a pew and am delighted to sit under the godly shepherd He has placed over me. I am to write this book and subsequent videos. And I am to find the highest mountaintop and proclaim His glory as loudly as possible. I am NO longer to be judgmental over the faith relationship between God and those that call on His name, but to allow Him that job as I simply proclaim!

I challenge you today to simply consider your own surrender, the condition of your heart. Are you willing to be molded into the "light" that Christ called us to be, or are you still holding a few things back, selfishly hoping that He will overlook the "treasures" that we are unwilling to let go of because I must tell you that anything less than 100% is unacceptable!

As for me—I am not there yet. I do not pretend that I am "better than thou". I am yet a sinner living in a sinful world, and as such, stumble and fall every step of the way. I see my shortcomings and failures every single day, and it grieves me that I am so unworthy of His love or attention, yet He continues to tap me on the shoulder and remind me that I am His.

He is asking you right now to surrender to His will for your life, to hold nothing back, and to let Him have it all so that He can continue the process of transforming your heart for His purpose. He wants you to be wholly devoted to Him and will accept nothing less than ALL of you.

Search your heart. What are you holding back? What have you been unwilling to sacrifice for His glory? What do you think you can accomplish that He cannot? Even the smallest, insignificant item will act as a roadblock to His glorification through you. Seek His face; seek His will for your life; submit to His authority over you, surrender to His will and He will change your heart forever. There is joy unimaginable on the other side of surrender. It is my solemn prayer that you can experience that joy.

May God keep you, bless you and, protect you.

Alone–Musing from September 10, 2010

Why does it seem I'm so alone?
Among the crowds, among the masses.
Not of it, yet still in a world,
I see not through rose-colored glasses.

So much has changed, so much is new,
Since, on my knees, I bowed to You.
I'm not myself; I'm not the same,
Sometimes I think I've gone insane.

The problems that I face each day,
They seem to me to be so heavy.
Yet You have told me You will stay,
And bear my burdens daily with me.

My friends, they do not yet discern,
Consoling with kind words and hugs.
They do not seem to understand,
The sacrifice which You demand.

No one, it seems, can comprehend,
The path I walk at Your command.
I realize now, this is not home.
A foreign land, condemned to roam.

I know it's for my own surrender,
The path to which Your hand is leading.
It's death to self that You desire,
In lessons now that You are teaching.

So, in You now will I find peace,
As well as lessons yet to learn.
Find joy fulfilling Your desire,
To be all Yours now I aspire.

They say the Christian walk is great,
That woe's and ill's You'll simply take.
I find it's not the walk that's grand,
But just the holding of Your hand.

So, take me now and make me Yours,
To You, I will surrender all.
Your perfect will complete in me,
And hold me when I fall.

CHAPTER 11

The Belt of Truth

> Webster's Dictionary definition of Truth: "the body of true statements and propositions; the property of being in accord with fact or reality."[12]

The Belt of Truth

A soldier's tunic was where his sword hung from and gave him freedom of movement. Much like the tactical vest modern soldiers and Police now use. The belt was the foundation of a soldier's armor, holding his sword and his breastplate. The belt was incredibly important.

The belt—this piece of armor is basic to all other pieces because truth and trustworthiness are essential to all the other qualities that believers need in order to withstand attacks.

The Roman Soldiers' Belt

The belt is where Roman soldiers stored their weapons. Without a belt, they could not carry a weapon! So, why does Paul associate the belt of a soldier with the truth? For Christians, God's Word is truth, and it serves as our foundation. The belt—known as the cingulum or

---

[12] Webster's Dictionary: https://www.merriam-webster.com/dictionary/ Viewed October 11, 2022

balteus—played a crucial role in the effectiveness of a soldier's armor. It was the belt that held the scabbard, without which there would be no place to put a sword. Imagine an overzealous soldier, fired up and charging out into battle, but without his belt, and consequently without a weapon!

In addition, the Nelson Study Bible says from the belt "hung strips of leather to protect the lower body." The Matthew Henry Commentary says the belt "girds on [secures] all the other pieces of our armor." Truth should cleave to us as a belt cleaves to our bodies.

Christ is our Source of Truth

Truth has been in short supply for millennia and especially so today, it would seem. Polls continue to show weakening support for our governmental leaders, social media sites, and news outlets. How much do you trust the information you receive and those who provide it?

We are told in Scripture that a fool is one who does not believe in the One True God and Scripture clearly tells us that if we do not believe in and are "of" God, then we are of our father the devil and full of lies and deceit.

> The fool says in his heart, There is no God. They are corrupt, they do abominable deeds; there is none who does good. The Lord looks down from heaven on the children of man, to see if there are any who understand and who seek after God. They have all turned aside; together they have become corrupt; there is none who does good, not even one. Have they no knowledge, all the evildoers who eat up my people as they eat bread and do not call upon the Lord? There they are in great terror, for God is with the generation of the righteous.
>
> Psalm 14:1-5

The Belt of Truth

> "I am the way, the truth, and the life."
>
> John 14:6

Remember, Satan is the father of lies. He disguises himself and manipulates your perspective. He wants to destroy you and your family. He wants to divide your home. He constantly reminds you of your past mistakes and bad choices. BUT—he cannot stand against the truth. Jesus said,

If you want VICTORY, you need to know the truth and the truth begins by understanding who you are in Christ Jesus.

> You are of your father the devil, and your will is to do your father's desires. He was a murderer from the beginning and does not stand in the truth, because there is no truth in him. When he lies, he speaks out of his own character, for he is a liar and the father of lies.
>
> John 8:44

What is truth

> Sanctify them by Your truth. Your word is truth.
>
> John 17:17

> Jesus, praying to the Father, gives a clear and straightforward definition of truth: God's Word. The Holy Bible (Scripture—the word of truth) was given by inspiration of God.
>
> 2 Timothy 3:16

The Greek expression translated "inspiration of God" literally means "God-breathed"! He actively and fully inspired the Bible to reveal His truth to us.

God's Truth

We have been created by God for truth and we are deceitful when we do not practice His truth. We become false witnesses (a VERY dangerous place to be by the way)

If we are truly His, we come to the light of His truth as found in His word (this is why we need to be students of the Bible). Truth is that which is consistent with the mind, will, character, glory, and being of God. Even more to the point: truth is the self-expression of God. That is the biblical meaning of truth. Because the definition of truth flows from God, truth is theological.

> You Desire Truth in the inner being and without God's truth, men will rise up to speak and speak become heretical (wrong) in their teaching.
>
> Psalm 51:6

> ... and from among your own selves' men will arise, speaking perverse things, to draw away the disciples after them.
>
> Acts 20:30

> If we say that we have fellowship with Him and yet walk in the darkness, we lie and do not practice the truth.
>
> Acts 20:30

> For the time is coming when people will not endure sound] teaching but having itching ears they will accumulate for themselves teachers to suit their own passions, will turn away from listening to the truth and wander off into myths. As for you, always be sober-minded, endure suffering, do the work of an evangelist, fulfill your ministry.
>
> 2 Timothy 4:3

> He who speaks truth tells what is right, But a false witness, deceit.

The Belt of Truth

Proverbs 12:17

As we continue to study His word and grow in our knowledge and faith, we continue to "grow in ALL aspects of Him who created us for truth." Truth means nothing apart from God. Truth cannot be adequately explained, recognized, understood, or defined without God as the source. Since He alone is eternal and self-existent and He alone is the Creator of all else, He is the fountain of all truth. When we seek God's truth in His word, creation, and Son we are honoring and glorifying Him who defines all truth.

> But he who practices the truth comes to the Light, so that his deeds may be manifested as having been wrought in God.
>
> John 3:21

> but we have renounced the things hidden because of shame, not walking in craftiness, or adulterating the word of God, but by the manifestation of truth commending ourselves to every man's conscience in the sight of God.
>
> 2 Corinthians 4:2

> but speaking the truth in love, we are to grow up in all aspects into Him who is the head, even Christ,
>
> Ephesians 4:15

We need to understand the truth of who God is—His character, and His faithfulness. We need to understand the truth of God's word.

> For the word of God is alive and active. Sharper than any double-edged sword, it penetrates even to dividing soul and spirit, joints, and marrow; it judges the thoughts and attitudes of the heart.
>
> Hebrews 4:12

Then, STAND in truth when you read God's word and speak life over yourself, your family, and your situation so that you too can find true freedom in Christ Jesus as I have recently.

> "Then you will know the truth, and the truth will set you free"
>
> John 8:32

> All Scripture is God-breathed and is useful for teaching, rebuking, correcting and training in righteousness. If our beliefs are not rooted in God's Word, we cannot expect to fight battles for Christ.
>
> 2 Timothy 3:16

Just as a belt is worn close to the body, we should hold God's truth close to us and allow it to surround us. When we remain in His word, we can distinguish what is true from what is untrue.

With this being said, I encourage you to apply the concept of the belt of truth to your life and hold onto God's truth. In the end, by remaining in His word, you will be equipped for spiritual battles that may come your way.

> His promises, His commands, His word—they are all truth, plain and simple. After all, The LORD of hosts has purposed, and who will annul it? His hand is stretched out, and who will turn it back? If God says something, there is no force that can stop Him from doing it—we can rest assured that it will be done.
>
> Isaiah 14:27

What does truth have to do with a belt?

> Test all things; hold fast what is good.
>
> 1 Thessalonians 5:21

The Belt of Truth

As Christians, we are to test all things and then hold on only to that which is good—the truth—discarding all else. We are to be like the Bereans who searched the Scriptures daily to find out whether these things were so.

Acts 17:11

If we are not convinced that our principles and beliefs are without exception 100% true, how can we expect to accomplish anything?

Have you "searched out" your Pastor for this Godly truth, or is there false teaching in his/her doctrine and preaching? What about the YouTube videos you watch? Are they Scripturally accurate and true to God's character and nature? The books you read? Friends you listen to? Remember Job's friends.

> Let not mercy and truth forsake you; bind them around your neck, write them on the tablet of your heart, and so find favor and high esteem in the sight of God and man.
>
> Proverbs 3:3-4

A belt encompasses the waist. Does our conviction in the truth encompass us? As the above scripture notes, truth must be bound around us and written on our hearts. Our conviction must reach beyond an outward show.

The belt used in Roman armor, as we have learned, provided a place for the soldier's sword. Our sword—the sword of the Spirit—likewise, needs a sheath. Truth is vital because, like a Roman soldier's belt, it allows us to carry the sword of the Spirit and use it effectively.

What other lessons can we learn from the biblical analogy of having our waist "girded" by a belt?

> Let your waist be girded and your lamps burning; and you yourselves be like men who wait for their master, when he will return from the wedding, that when he comes and knocks, they may open to him immediately. Blessed are those servants whom the master, when he comes, will find

> watching. Assuredly, I say to you that he will gird himself
> and have them sit down to eat and will come and serve them.
>
> Luke 12:35-37

Christ told us to always be watching and ready for His return.

> Therefore gird up the loins of your mind, be sober, and
> rest your hope fully upon the grace that is to be brought
> to you at the revelation of Jesus Christ.
>
> 1 Peter 1:13

Peter used an interesting analogy: "Gird up the loins of your mind." This implies tucking in long garments to be ready to move quickly. The New International Version translates it as "prepare your minds for action."

What are the dangers of not wearing the belt?

> And do not be conformed to this world, but be transformed
> by the renewing of your mind, that you may prove what is
> that good and acceptable and perfect will of God.
>
> Romans 12:2

The world we live in teaches that truth is what we make it, that good and bad are relative, and that there are no absolutes, only equally valid opinions. But the Bible teaches that truth is God's word—that good and bad are defined by Him and that there are eternal and unchangeable absolutes, uninfluenced by opinions. Paul wrote to the Romans telling them to "not be conformed to this world." Part of that means not buying into a system of belief that says absolute truth is a myth. As Christians, we know both that there is truth and that it is absolute.

> Be diligent to present yourself approved to God, a worker
> who does not need to be ashamed, rightly dividing the
> word of truth.
>
> 2 Timothy 2:15

The Belt of Truth

Imagine a belt with a segment missing. No matter how tiny the sliver isn't there, the belt is still useless. To do its job, it must be one continuous, unbroken piece. Now, imagine living a way of life you don't completely agree with. Maybe it doesn't seem like a big deal—after all, what are a couple minor points that you're not sure about? They are everything. To try to live God's way without total belief in its validity is like trying to hold your sword up with a belt that isn't continuous. Neither will work. Our trust in God and His Word must be solid, without break, or else we will quickly find ourselves without a weapon. No matter how effective the rest of our armor is, we are useless without our swords. We need to be rightly dividing the word of truth—knowing what we believe, and why.

So, how secure is your belt?

Satan's Meeting 7:

> When we stray from the truth, we become distracted from the things of God and become lost. Satan called a worldwide convention. In his opening address to his demons, he said, "We can't keep the Christians from going to church. We can't keep them from reading their Bibles and knowing the truth. We can't even keep them from biblical values. But we can do something else. We can keep them from forming an intimate, continual experience with Christ.

"If they gain that connection with Jesus, our power over them is broken. So let them go to church, let them have their Christian lifestyles, but steal their time so they can't gain that experience with Jesus Christ.

"This is what I want you to do. Distract them from gaining hold of their Savior and maintaining that vital connection throughout their day."

"How shall we do this?" asked his demons.

"Keep them busy with the nonessentials of life and invest

unnumbered schemes to occupy their minds," he answered. "Tempt them to spend, spend, spend, then borrow, borrow, borrow. Convince them to work six or seven days a week, 10-12 hours a day, so they can afford their lifestyles. Keep them from spending time with their children. As their families fragment, soon their homes will offer no escape from the pressures of work.

"Overstimulate their minds so they cannot hear that still small voice. Entice them to play the radio or CD player wherever they drive, to keep the TV, the DVD player, and their CDs going constantly in their homes. Fill their coffee tables with magazines and newspapers. Pound their minds with news 24 hours a day. Invade their driving moments with billboards. Flood their mailboxes and e-mail with junk, sweepstakes, and every kind of newsletter and promotion.

"Even in their recreation, let them be excessive. Have them return from their holidays exhausted, disquieted, and unprepared for the coming week. And when they gather for spiritual fellowship, involve them in gossip and small talk so they leave with souls unfulfilled.

"Let them be involved in evangelism. But crowd their lives with so many good causes that they have no time to seek power from Christ. Soon they will be working in their own strength, sacrificing their health, and family unity for the good of the cause."

It was quite a convention. And the demons went eagerly to their assignments. Has the devil been successful in his scheme? You be the judge. Are you tired? Worn out? Burned out on religion?

> Come to me. Get away with me and you'll recover your life. I'll show you how to take a real rest. Walk with me and work with me—watch how I do it. Learn the unforced rhythms of grace. I won't lay anything heavy or ill-fitting on you. Keep company with me and you'll learn to live freely and lightly.
>
> Matthew 11:28-30

CHAPTER 12

The Breastplate of Righteousness

Finally, be strong in the Lord and in the strength of his might. Put on the whole armor of God, so that you may be able to stand against the schemes of the devil. For we do not wrestle against flesh and blood, but against the rulers, against the authorities, against the cosmic powers over this present darkness, against the spiritual forces of evil in the heavenly places. Therefore, take up the whole armor of God, that you may be able to withstand in the evil day, and having done all, to stand firm. Stand therefore, having fastened on the belt of truth, and having put on the breastplate of righteousness, and, as shoes for your feet, having put on the readiness given by the gospel of peace. In all circumstances take up the shield of faith, with which you can extinguish all the flaming darts of the evil one; and take the helmet of salvation, and the sword of the Spirit, which is the word of God, always praying in the Spirit, with all prayer and supplication. To that end keep alert with all perseverance, making supplication for all the saints, and for me, that words may be given to me in opening my mouth boldly to proclaim the mystery of the gospel.

Ephesians 6:10-19

What is this Breastplate that Paul is referring to in this passage? What is its purpose, how was it worn, and what type of protection did it offer? It primarily protected the internal organs which at the time were the seat of the various human emotions.

The heart was the center of affection, the spleen was the seat of passion and emotion, courage originated in the stomach, the head (brain) was the author of wisdom, the kidneys produced affection, melancholy (sadness) found its roots in the bile, mercy was to be found in the bowels (of all places), and a person's spirit was thought to reside in the blood.

Notice the connection between the blood and the heart –They believed that the spirit (the blood) was pumped throughout the body by the center of human emotion (the heart). There seems, in this belief, to be a critical link between our souls and our emotions. When we experience a powerful emotion, fear, anger, grief, and love, adrenaline pours into the blood, increases the blood pressure, and accelerates the heart. It made perfect sense for the ancients to believe that the heart-controlled emotion.

Even today we use numerous expressions that indicate the heart is the center of emotion." Affairs of the heart", "to break one's heart", "from the depths of the heart", "heart is in the right place", to "wear one's heart on their sleeve", to "take to heart", to "pull on one's heartstrings", to "set one's heart" upon a goal.

This idea of our emotions originating in the organs does indeed have some Biblical basis.

> I bless the Lord who gives me counsel; in the night also, my heart instructs me.
>
> Psalm 16:7

The Hebrew word for heart in this passage is literally translated as "kidney."

> And Joseph made haste; for his bowels did yearn upon his brother: and he sought where to weep; and he entered into

The Breastplate of Righteousness

his chamber and wept there. And he washed his face, and went out, and refrained himself, and said, Set on bread.

Genesis 43:29-31 (KJV)

Have you ever received good news about a situation where you thought hope was lost?

Famine was in the land. People were in desperate need of food, facing starvation. Joseph was at this point the second most powerful man in the kingdom, second only to Pharaoh, and yet his heart ached for his father and brother Benjamin whom he had not seen since his capture by his brothers. Joseph was so overcome with emotion that he had to remove himself from the scene and take a moment of privacy to weep—and to get himself back under control.

> "But what comes out of the mouth proceeds from the heart, and this defiles a person. For out of the heart come evil thoughts, murder, adultery, sexual immorality, theft, false witness, slander."
>
> Matthew 15:18-19
>
> "You shall love the Lord your God with all your heart . . ."
>
> Matthew 22:37

Scripture is rife with references to the connection between the heart and our emotions, thoughts, and feelings.

> And I will give you a new heart, and a new spirit I will put within you. And I will remove the heart of stone from your flesh and give you a heart of flesh.
>
> Ezekiel 36:26

Evil stems from a "heart of stone" as we are born into sin with, and the "righteous" thoughts come from the "heart of flesh" given us in Salvation.

In short, the Breastplate of Righteousness protects the centers of emotion and in wearing this righteousness we can stand rightly when the daily events of our lives tempt us into sliding back into the thoughts and emotions of our formerly unsaved "hearts of stone."

"Having put on the Breastplate of Righteousness"

"Having put on . . ." This text is in the past tense—an event that already happened and not having to be repeated. We are to put on this righteousness once and are to always wear it. "Breastplate"—as we have already seen the breastplate covers and protects the vital organs that support and sustain life. Should any of these organs be damaged or destroyed, life would cease. Spiritually speaking, the breastplate covers and protects the centers of our emotions and keeps us from falling into the temptations of sin and unrighteousness.

Righteousness

Righteousness vs. Unrighteousness

> Webster's Dictionary defines righteousness as behavior that is "acting in accord with divine or moral law and free from guilt or sin."[13]

This is behavior, which is moral, ethical, virtuous, or noble.

They go on to say that all of these behavioral traits stem from a sense of rightness, fairness, equity, moral excellence of character, guiltlessness, and blamelessness—freedom from anything petty, mean, or dubious in conduct or character.

What does Scripture say about "Righteousness"?

Righteousness is one of the attributes of God. Its chief meaning concerns ethical conduct. The ways of righteousness are plain and safe and in them, we may find a "holy security" while the ways of

---

[13] Webster's Dictionary: https://www.merriam-webster.com/dictionary/ Viewed October 11, 2022

The Breastplate of Righteousness

wickedness are dangerous and those who indulge themselves in sin are fitting themselves for destruction.

Biblical Righteousness

> For those who live according to the flesh set their minds on the things of the flesh, but those who live according to the Spirit set their minds on the things of the Spirit. For to set the mind on the flesh is death, but to set the mind on the Spirit is life and peace. For the mind that is set on the flesh is hostile to God, for it does not submit to God's law; indeed, it cannot. Those who are in the flesh cannot please God. You, however, are not in the flesh but in the Spirit, if in fact the Spirit of God dwells in you. Anyone who does not have the Spirit of Christ does not belong to him. But if Christ is in you, although the body is dead because of sin, the Spirit is life because of righteousness.
>
> Romans 8:5

From the above passage, we see that the wicked person makes 'self' the goal, following a mere shadow which in the end eludes his grasp, while the righteous one (in Christ) lives altogether for his God and will have a sure reward, promised, and certain! The one who is "unrighteous" seeks happiness and hopes to find it in the path which they have marked out for themselves, but "they work a deceitful work," which invariably disappoints their hopes.

Whatever the gratification afforded them, it is transient and brings no solid satisfaction with it. Whether their pursuit is more sensual, or more refined, it still leaves in the bosom an aching void, which the world can never fill. Solomon tried everything that was within the reach of mortal man, intellectual as well as sensual; and, after a full experience of it all, declared it all to be "vanity and vexation of spirit." The one who is "righteous" sows seeds that may lie a long time under the dirt and may seem as if buried forever: but they shall spring up in due season and bring with it a harvest of solid joy.

Scripture attests to this.

"The work of righteousness is peace," and that, "in keeping of God's commandments there is great reward."

This "reward is sure" on two accounts:

> It is independent of all activity and behavior, and it is secured to him by the promise of God himself. Happiness that comes from earthly things may be destroyed by disease, accident, or pains of the body and mind. Spiritual happiness is independent of all these things and often derives a zest from those very things which seem most calculated to subvert it. If we look to a future state, where the wicked, notwithstanding all their neglect of heavenly things, hope to have a portion with the righteous, we shall see the text fulfilled to all its extent. What surprise and anguish will seize hold upon the wicked the very instant he opens his eyes in the eternal world! Conceive of "the rich man" summoned from his carnal indulgences into the presence of his God: how little did he imagine but a few days before what such a life would issue! How deceitful had his work been, and how elusive all his hopes! But the righteous is sure to find his hopes realized, and his highest expectations infinitely exceeded: for God's express determination is, that.

Galatians 6:7-8; "Do not be deceived: God is not mocked, for whatever one sows, that will he also reap. For the one who sows to his own flesh will from the flesh reap corruption, but the one who sows to the Spirit will from the Spirit reap eternal life."

The Breastplate of Righteousness

Be "Pure and Holy"

> Rejoice in the Lord always; again, I will say, rejoice. Let your reasonableness be known to everyone. The Lord is at hand; do not be anxious about anything, but in everything by prayer and supplication with thanksgiving let your requests be made known to God. And the peace of God, which surpasses all understanding, will guard your hearts and your minds in Christ Jesus. Finally, brothers, whatever is true, whatever is honorable, whatever is just, whatever is pure, whatever is lovely, whatever is commendable, if there is any excellence, if there is anything worthy of praise, think about these things. What you have learned and received and heard and seen in me—practice these things, and the God of peace will be with you.
>
> Philippians 4:4-9

Righteousness then, is the act of behaving in a manner that is ethically, morally, and spiritually upright—practicing those things that are pure and holy in God's sight and abstaining from behavior that is worldly, self-centered, and wicked in God's sight. To be righteous means that we are to exhibit thoughts and behaviors that are pleasing to God and shun those that displease Him.

God, in Jesus Christ, will guard our hearts and our minds if we think about and practice that which is just, pure, lovely, commendable, excellent, and worthy of praise.

We are to practice those things that are evidenced in Christ Jesus as displayed in the daily life of Paul the Apostle. So, to behave righteously means that we are to practice all things that are pure, lovely, commendable, excellent, and worthy of praise. But how can we know exactly the type of behavior that is exhibited by "pure and holy" motives?

We look generally to Scripture and more specifically to Christ Himself for the answer. It is His life we are to emulate, His behaviors which should be our standard, His righteousness that should be our trademark.

What does the Bible teach us about the behavior and attitudes of righteous men so that we may emulate them?

> "If you keep My commandments, you will abide in My love; just as I have kept My Father's commandments and abide in His love"
>
> John 15:10

Follow Christ's example in all things

> "Everyone who comes to Me and hears My words and Acts on them, I will show you whom he is like he is like a man building a house, who dug deep and laid a foundation on the rock; and when a flood occurred, the torrent burst against that house and could not shake it, because it had been well built."
>
> Luke 6:47-48

We need to fervently read, know, and obey Scripture.

> Thus, Noah did—according to all that God had commanded him to do.
>
> Genesis 6:22

> He did right in the sight of the Lord, according to all that his father David had done.
>
> 2 Kings 18:3

Surround yourself and spend quality time with true Godly men and women. It is said and is utterly true that we will eventually become like those with whom we associate. In my particular case, I now need to surround myself with Christ as I'll soon be with Him.

> The Lord said to Satan, "Have you considered my servant job? For there is no one like him on the earth, a blameless and upright man, fearing God and turning away from evil"
>
> Job 1:8

Our behavior is reflective of our devotion.

> But his delight is in the law of the Lord, and in His law, he meditates day and night.
>
> Psalm 1:2

Always meditate on Scripture. Extreme? Possibly. Commanded? Definitely!

> How blessed are those whose way is blameless, Who walk in the law of the LORD. How blessed are those who observe His testimonies, Who seek Him with all their heart. They also do no unrighteousness; They walk in His ways.
>
> Psalm 119:1-4

Seek God and His statutes above all else. Make Him first in all things. Every desire should be weighed against His desires. Every decision is based upon His will.

> Now for this very reason also, applying all diligence, in your faith supplies moral excellence, and in your moral excellence, knowledge, and in your knowledge, self-control, and in your self-control, perseverance, and in perseverance, godliness, and in your godliness, brotherly kindness, and in your brotherly kindness, love. For if these qualities are yours and are increasing, they render

you neither useless nor unfruitful in the true knowledge of our Lord Jesus Christ. For he who lacks these qualities is blind or short-sighted, having forgotten his purification from his former sins. Therefore, brethren, be all the more diligent to make certain about His calling and choosing you; for as long as you practice these things, you will never stumble; for in this way the entrance into the eternal kingdom of our Lord and Savior Jesus Christ will be abundantly supplied to you.

2 Peter 1:5-11

There is certainly no shortage of scripture that gives us how we are to think, behave and act righteously. If we simply take some of these out of scripture and begin to develop a list of the character traits and actions of a righteous man or woman.

A righteous man or woman

Does not act unbecomingly (1 Corinthians 13:5), does not seek his or her own agenda, is not provoked (into anger), does not take into account wrong suffering (forgiving), approves the things that are excellent, remains sincere and blameless, acts in a disciplined manner, is above reproach (without guilt), is the husband to wife of one husband or wife, is temperate of emotion, is prudent, respectable, hospitable, Reverent, is not malicious or gossiping, is sober-minded, seeks the things above, loves Christ more than self or family, walks by the Spirit, and does not satisfy the desires of the flesh.

Keep His commandments (we need to know them to keep them)

Remember too that while we are commanded to walk righteously as disciples of Jesus Christ, it is not our own righteousness that saves us but Christ's righteousness that we receive through faith in His redeeming work at the Cross and in Christ's righteousness, we walk in the light instead of in the darkness of sin and wickedness.

The Breastplate of Righteousness

This is the message we have heard from him and proclaim to you, that God is light, and in him is no darkness at all. If we say we have fellowship with him while we walk in darkness, we lie and do not practice the truth. But if we walk in the light, as he is in the light, we have fellowship with one another, and the blood of Jesus his Son cleanses us from all sin. If we say we have no sin, we deceive ourselves, and the truth is not in us. If we confess our sins, he is faithful and just to forgive us our sins and to cleanse us from all unrighteousness. If we say we have not sinned, we make him a liar, and his word is not in us.

1 John 1:5-10

The Breastplate of Righteousness is the behavior that keeps our hearts pure, but it is not behavior that originates of our own accord. It is the behavior that is reflective of and authored by, the Holy Spirit that has been promised to all who are truly Christ's and seek to serve only Him.

"But seek first the kingdom of God and his righteousness,"

Matthew 6:33a

CHAPTER 13

The Gospel of Peace

Finally, be strong in the Lord and in the strength of his might. Put on the whole armor of God, that you may be able to stand against the schemes of the devil. For we do not wrestle against flesh and blood, but against the rulers, against the authorities, against the cosmic powers over this present darkness, against the spiritual forces of evil in the heavenly places. Therefore, take up the whole armor of God, that you may be able to withstand in the evil day, and having done all, to stand firm. Stand therefore, having fastened on the belt of truth, and having put on the breastplate of righteousness, and, as shoes for your feet, having put on the readiness given by the gospel of peace. In all circumstances take up the shield of faith, with which you can extinguish all the flaming darts of the evil one; and take the helmet of salvation, and the sword of the Spirit, which is the word of God, always praying in the Spirit, with all prayer and supplication. To that end keep alert with all perseverance, making supplication for all the saints, and also for me, that words may be given to me in opening my mouth boldly to proclaim the mystery of the gospel.

Ephesians 6:10-19

The Christ in my Cancer

Introduction & Historical Context

What does Paul mean when he says, "The Readiness given by the Gospel of peace"?

Traditional Roman Shoes—What are their purpose, how were they worn, and what type of protection did they offer? Are they offensive or defensive in intent?

The shoes of a Roman soldier were designed primarily for the protection and stability of the soldier. They were more like "half boots" rather than shoes as they rose about midway up the calf and had leather straps that could be tightened around the lower leg, thus securing them to the wearer.

Much like the studded cleats of a football player today, the Roman boots were constructed of a heavy durable material designed for strength. At the time, this was heavy leather. The soles were constructed of a thick, hard leather usually about ¾" thick, and were studded with hollow nail-like spikes. These spikes provided traction during the battle where, in hand-to-hand combat, radical turns and steps were to be expected.

The soldiers would often wrap their legs with a cotton cloth under the leather straps of the shoes to provide support for the ankles and lower legs much like a boxer wraps his wrists before donning his boxing gloves.

Imagine a pro football player going into the game barefoot. How long would he last before being injured beyond his ability to play? How ridiculous would this look to the other players of both teams? Even better, imagine that same player wearing a loose-fitting pair of slippers onto the field. How long until his ankles are shattered? How long until he is "tripped up" and becomes not only useless in the battle, but also a hindrance to the other players on the field?

The shoes of the Gospel mentioned here by Paul serve very much the same purposes. They keep us stable and secure when in our spiritual battles, and they protect us from a catastrophic injury that would "take us out" of the battle.

The Gospel of Peace

He will guard the feet of his faithful ones, but the wicked shall be cut off in darkness, for not by might shall a man prevail.

1 Samuel 2:9

When I thought, My foot slips, your steadfast love, O Lord, held me up.

Psalm 94:18

Doctrinally weak Christians are easily "tripped up" by the devil. In short, adorning and properly wearing the shoes of the Gospel of Peace begins with truth.

Knowledge of Biblical truth, a conviction of this Biblical truth, and proper doctrine (a proper Christian worldview). Paul is basically telling us in this passage, "Prepare yourselves with proper doctrine and go—share it."

Definitions

"Having put on . . ."

As before, this is in the past tense—an event that already happened and not having to be repeated. We are to put on these shoes once and are to always wear them.

It must also be noted that the term "put on" implies that this is an act that we alone can complete. There will be no one else to do this for us. Husbands, during battle, your wives are not likely going to come to your bedside in the morning and put your boots on for you!

"Readiness": Another word would be Preparation. A State of readiness equipped and established implies that this was completed before the battle.

"Gospel": What exactly is the Gospel?

The word Gospel actually translates as "Good News" or "Glad Tidings."

> Webster's Dictionary defines "Gospel" as "The message concerning Christ, the kingdom of God, and salvation."[14]

The Gospel is absolutely necessary for both Salvation AND victory in the Christian life.

It is not a feeling! It is the summation of the facts and truth regarding Jesus Christ and is rooted in the life, work, and person of God's only Son.

"Peace": What does Paul mean here when he uses the term "peace"?

Could he mean happiness? Peace with our neighbors? Our co-workers? Our enemies?

There are two dimensions to this peace that Paul is herein referring to. Vertical Peace is through the Gospel we come to have Peace with God. Horizontal Peace is the same Gospel that brings us to a state of peace with other believers.

Note that I did not say, "other Christians." It is not about the label that we wear but about the condition of our hearts and the state of our surrender to Christ. Many who claim the title of "Christian" are, unfortunately, in error concerning their relationship with Him.

> Therefore, remember that at one time you Gentiles in the flesh, called 'the uncircumcision' by what is called the circumcision, which is made in the flesh by hands—remember that you were at that time separated from Christ, alienated from the commonwealth of Israel and strangers to the covenants of promise, having no hope and without God in the world. But now in Christ Jesus you who once were far off have been brought near by the blood of Christ. For he himself is our peace, who has made us both one and has broken down in his flesh the dividing wall of hostility by abolishing the law of commandments

---

14 Webster's Dictionary: https://www.merriam-webster.com/dictionary/ Viewed October 11, 2022

expressed in ordinances, that he might create in himself one new man in place of the two, so making peace, and might reconcile us both to God in one body through the cross, thereby killing the hostility. And he came and preached peace to you who were far off and peace to those who were near. For through him we both have access in one Spirit to the Father. So then you are no longer strangers and aliens, but you are fellow citizens with the saints and members of the household of God, built on the foundation of the apostles and prophets, Christ Jesus himself being the cornerstone, in whom the whole structure, being joined together, grows into a holy temple in the Lord. In him you also are being built together into a dwelling place for God by the Spirit.

For this reason, I, Paul, a prisoner for Christ Jesus on behalf of you Gentiles—assuming that you have heard of the stewardship of God's grace that was given to me for you, how the mystery was made known to me by revelation, as I have written briefly. When you read this, you can perceive my insight into the mystery of Christ, which was not made known to the sons of men in other generations as it has now been revealed to his holy apostles and prophets by the Spirit. This mystery is that the Gentiles are fellow heirs, members of the same body, and partakers of the promise in Christ Jesus through the gospel. Of this gospel I was made a minister according to the gift of God's grace, which was given me by the working of his power. To me, though I am the very least of all the saints, this grace was given, to preach to the Gentiles the unsearchable riches of Christ, and to bring to light for everyone what is the plan of the mystery hidden for ages in God who created all things, so that through the church the manifold wisdom of God might now be made known to the rulers and authorities in the heavenly places. This was according to the eternal purpose that he has realized in Christ Jesus our Lord, in whom we have boldness and access with confidence through our faith in him. So, I ask you not to lose heart over what I am suffering for you, which is your glory.

Ephesians 2:11-3:13

Without Peace: Verses 11 and 12 from the above passage defines our condition before we experience and are transformed through the Gospel. We are uncircumcised and separated from Christ—alienated from the commonwealth, strangers to the covenant of promise, ignorant of the salvation message, without hope, and without God in the world.

Verse 13, however, gives us hope and "peace"

We are brought near by the blood of Christ; Christ is our peace. This is kind of the point of the whole message. We are made one, the division of hostility has been removed, we are reconciled to God, and we (all believers) are now one body.

Vertical Peace

For he himself is our peace. It is through Christ that we are reconciled to God!

> ... and through him to reconcile to himself all things, whether on earth or in heaven, making peace by the blood of his cross. And you, who once were alienated and hostile in mind, doing evil deeds, he has now reconciled in his body of flesh by his death, in order to present you holy and blameless and above reproach before him ...
>
> Colossians 1:20-22

Therefore, since we have been justified by faith, we have peace with God through our Lord Jesus Christ.

Romans 5:1

The Gospel of Peace

Since, therefore, we have now been justified by his blood, much more shall we be saved by him from the wrath of God. For if while we were enemies we were reconciled to God by the death of his Son, much more, now that we are reconciled, shall we be saved by his life. More than that, we also rejoice in God through our Lord Jesus Christ, through whom we have now received reconciliation.

Romans 5:9-11

Horizontal Peace

Peace with fellow followers of Christ:

Through Christ, we are no longer strangers and aliens, but fellow citizens with the saints and members of the household of God! We are one in Christ. There is no room in this for even one iota of elitism or prejudice in Christ! We are to be messengers of this Gospel of peace.

Go on up to a high mountain, O Zion, herald of good news; lift up your voice with strength, O Jerusalem, herald of good news; lift it up, fear not; say to the cities of Judah, Behold your God!

Isaiah 40:9

How beautiful upon the mountains are the feet of him who brings good news, who publishes peace, who brings good news of happiness, who publishes salvation, who says to Zion, Your God reigns. The voice of your watchmen—they lift up their voice; together they sing for joy; for eye to eye they see.

Isaiah 52:7-8

Who has believed what he has heard from us? And to whom has the arm of the Lord been revealed?

Isaiah 53:1

> "Peace, peace, to the far and to the near," says the Lord, "and I will heal him. But the wicked are like the tossing sea; for it cannot be quiet, and its waters toss up mire and dirt. There is no peace," says my God, "for the wicked." True and False Fasting "Cry aloud; do not hold back; lift up your voice like a trumpet; declare to my people their transgression, to the house of Jacob their sins."
>
> Isaiah 57:19-58:1

The Necessity of the Holy Spirit in this proclamation

> The Spirit of the Lord God is upon me, because the Lord has anointed me to bring good news to the poor; he has sent me to bind up the brokenhearted, to proclaim liberty to the captives, and the opening of the prison to those who are bound; to proclaim the year of the Lord's favor, and the day of vengeance of our God; to comfort all who mourn; to grant to those who mourn in Zion—to give them a beautiful headdress instead of ashes, the oil of gladness instead of mourning, the garment of praise instead of a faint spirit.
>
> Isaiah 61:1-3

Always be ready to share the "Good News"

> I charge you in the presence of God and of Christ Jesus, who is to judge the living and the dead, and by his appearing and his kingdom: preach the word; be ready in season and out of season; reprove, rebuke, and exhort, with complete patience and teaching. For the time is coming when people will not endure sound teaching but having itching ears they will accumulate for themselves teachers to suit their own passions, and will turn away from listening to the truth and wander off into myths. As

for you, always be sober-minded, endure suffering, do the work of an evangelist, fulfill your ministry.

2 Timothy 4:1-5

Understand the necessity of this Gospel of Peace

This Jesus is the stone that was rejected by you, the builders, which has become the cornerstone. And there is salvation in no one else, for there is no other name under heaven given among men by which we must be saved.

Acts 4:11-12

In this message, be bold, confident, and unashamed

For I am not ashamed of the gospel, for it is the power of God for salvation to everyone who believes, to the Jew first and to the Greek. For in it the righteousness of God is revealed from faith for faith, as it is written, "The righteous shall live by faith."

Romans 1:16-17

Make sure that you are properly equipped—Always being students of the cross.

"Fear not, therefore; you are of more value than many sparrows. So, everyone who acknowledges me before men, I also will acknowledge before my Father who is in heaven, but whoever denies me before men, I also will deny before my Father who is in heaven."

Matthew 10:22

Be constantly ready to preach and witness. Be clearly heard. Stand on a mountaintop when you proclaim the Gospel and do not hide the message under a basket. Be authoritative.

We have a message of salvation regarding our salvation given by eternal condemnation from the creator of all life. We should proclaim this as if we believe it. Remember, there is no other name. Be intensely positive, we share the Gospel of peace, not condemnation. Put all judgment and elitism aside! Be deeply persuaded of the necessity of the message! Again, there is salvation in no other name than Jesus Christ.

Salvation is By Grace Alone, Through Faith Alone, In Christ Alone!

The message we share is not A Gospel. It is THE Gospel! Finally, always be purposefully advancing. In other words—Go! Remember, our shoes are made of the absolute best material available in all of creation. Wear them with confidence and courage!

Charles Haddon Spurgeon speaks on this in *Shoes for Pilgrims and Warriors*: "The Christian was evidently intended to be in motion, for here are shoes for his feet. His head is provided with a helmet, for he is to be thoughtful. His heart is covered with a breastplate, for he is to be a man of feeling. His whole nature is protected by a shield, for he is called to endurance and caution. And that he is to be active is certain, for a sword is provided for his hand to use and sandals with which his feet are to be shod. To suppose that a Christian is to be motionless as a post and inanimate as a stone, or merely pensive as a weeping willow and passive as a reed shaken by the wind, is altogether a mistake! God works in us and His grace is the great motive power which secures our salvation, but He does not so work in us as to chloroform us into unconscious submission, or engineer us into mechanical motion—He orchestrates all our activities by working in us "to will and to do of His good pleasure." Grace imparts healthy life and life rejoices in activity! The Lord never intended His people to be automatons worked by clockwork, or cold and dead statues—He meant them to have life, to have it abundantly— and in the power of that life to be full of energy! It is true He makes us lie down in green pastures, but equally certain is it that He leads us onward beside the still waters! A true believer is an active person—he has feet and uses them.

Now, he who marches meets with stones, or if as a warrior he dashes into the thick of the conflict he is assailed with weapons and, therefore, he needs to be suitably shod to meet his perils. The active and energetic Christian meets with temptations which do not happen to others. Idle persons can scarcely be said to be in danger—they are a stage beyond that and are already overcome! Satan scarcely needs to tempt them—they rather tempt him and are a fermenting mass in which sin exceedingly multiplies—a decaying body around which the vultures of vice are sure to gather. But earnest laborious believers are sure to be assailed, even as fruit bearing trees are certain to be visited by the birds. Satan cannot stand a man who earnestly serves God—he does damage to the archenemy's dominions and, therefore, he must be incessantly assailed. The prince of darkness will try, if he can, to injure the good man's character, to break his communion with God, to spoil the simplicity of his faith, to make him proud of what he is doing, or to make him despair of success. In some way or other he will, if possible, bruise the worker's heel or trip him up, or lame him altogether. Because of all these dangers, infinite mercy has provided gospel shoes for the believer's feet—shoes of the best kind—such as only those warriors wear who serve the Lord of hosts!

We believe in a gospel which was formed in the purpose of God from all eternity, designed with infinite wisdom, worked out at an enormous expense, costing nothing less than the blood of Jesus, brought home by infinite power, even by the might of the Holy Spirit! It is a gospel full of blessings, any one of which would outweigh a world in price—a gospel as free as it is full, a gospel everlasting and immutable, a gospel of which we can never think too much, whose praises we can never exaggerate! It is from this choice gospel that its choicest essence is taken, namely, its peace. And from this peace those sandals are prepared with which a man may tread on the lion and the adder, yes, and on the fierce burning coals of malice, slander and persecution! What better shoes can our souls require?

Let this suffice concerning these shoes, but a serious question suggests itself to me. Are there not some of you who have to travel to eternity and yet have no shoes for the journey? How can the unconverted man hope to reach heaven when he has no shoes on his feet? How will he bear the troubles of life, the temptations of the flesh and the trials of death? I pray you, unconverted ones, look at yourselves and at the way—and see how impossible it is for you to accomplish the journey unless you go to Jesus

The Christ in my Cancer

and obtain from Him the grace which will make you pilgrims to glory! Go, I pray you, and find peace in Him—and then your life journey shall be happy and safe, and the end eternal joy—for your feet will be shod with 'the preparation of the gospel of peace.'"[15]

---

[15] Spurgeon, C. H. (n.d.), *Shoes for Pilgrims and Warriors* https://www.spurgeongems.org/sermon/chs3143.pdf. Viewed Retrieved October 11, 2022

CHAPTER 14

The Shield of Faith

Finally, be strong in the Lord and in the strength of his might. Put on the whole armor of God, that you may be able to stand against the schemes of the devil. For we do not wrestle against flesh and blood, but against the rulers, against the authorities, against the cosmic powers over this present darkness, against the spiritual forces of evil in the heavenly places. Therefore, take up the whole armor of God, that you may be able to withstand in the evil day, and having done all, to stand firm. Stand therefore, having fastened on the belt of truth, and having put on the breastplate of righteousness, and, as shoes for your feet, having put on the readiness given by the gospel of peace. In all circumstances take up the shield of faith, with which you can extinguish all the flaming darts of the evil one; and take the helmet of salvation, and the sword of the Spirit, which is the word of God, praying at all times in the Spirit, with all prayer and supplication. To that end keep alert with all perseverance, making supplication for all the saints, and also for me, that words may be given to me in opening my mouth boldly to proclaim the mystery of the gospel

Ephesians 6:10-19

The Armor

There are six pieces of armor/weaponry mentioned in this passage.

Paul is using an example from the Roman military to give those to whom he was writing a clear understanding of the pieces of armor and for what each was to be used. He uses examples that they would easily understand. Part of our understanding then should also be to understand the armor worn by the Roman soldiers and what each was for.

The first three were the most time-consuming to put on and were therefore always worn whether in battle or at rest. They were never removed until the battle was won, and the soldier was safely back in his own land. These are: The Belt of Truth (Commitment), The Breastplate of Righteousness (Holiness), and The Shoes of the Gospel of Peace (Confidence).

The remaining three pieces were easier to remove and so were removed during times when the battle was not happening but was always kept close at hand and available for immediate use. These are: The Shield of Faith, The Helmet of Salvation, and The Sword of the Spirit.

Think about a baseball player. He does not take off his uniform or his shoes as long as the game is being played, but he does set his cap and bat down nearby until they are needed. Once it is his "time to do battle." he picks up his weapons and enters the fray. There were no hard and fast rules for how to wear the armor needed, and no punishment doled out for its inappropriate use was necessary.

It was a matter of life and death. If you wanted to survive in the battle, you went to the greatest effort to not only know exactly how to apply the armor but also wanted to be well trained in its use. This armor quite literally meant the difference between survival (victory) and defeat (death).

We have already covered the Helmet of Salvation. Now we are going to discuss the Shield of Faith and its role in the battle we find ourselves in and, boy oh boy are we in the midst of a battle!

In ALL Circumstances Take up The Shield of Faith

The Shield of Faith

History of the Roman Shield

There were two shields carried by the Roman Soldiers in AD 60-62 when this Epistle was written by Paul from prison.

The first was a small round shield with two leather straps on the back so that the soldier could hold it with his free hand while swinging a small dagger-like sword with the other. This shield was meant for close, hand-to-hand combat but would be utterly ineffective on the open battlefield and would have little effect at stopping the flaming arrows spoken of here in this passage.

The second shield (a Roman Scutum) used by Roman soldiers was much larger and thicker and provide a much greater degree of protection. It was integral to the configuration of the Testudo, or Tortoise, formation in which several soldiers would stand or kneel closely together and collectively use their shields to form a tortoise-like shell around them, thus creating an impenetrable covering that offered protection to the entire group. Notice the greater degree of protection offered by this "group" strategy as opposed to the limited coverage area the shield would provide in its solitary use by an individual. Do you think there is a reason that Paul is using this shield as an example for us as a "body" of believers?

Do we stand better protected on our own or are we better able to defend against the attacks of our common enemy as a larger group acting in unison? Remember, this is a battle to the death we are involved in. It is NOT a video game that we can reset when we fall, nor is it a proxy war that is happening halfway around the world so that we can detach ourselves from the ugly reality of it.

The enemy of our very souls wants to destroy us and is willing to use any means necessary to that end. Would it not be wise for us to put our petty little differences aside so that we can work and stand united together under the "Testudo" of Faith so that we might all be victorious?

This shield weighed about 22 pounds and measured about 4 1/2 feet high by 2 1/2 feet wide by 2 inches thick. It was bordered with a ring of brass which added structural integrity and strength. The Scutum was often covered in oil-soaked leather which would extinguish the flaming arrows that were being fired at them "En Mass". The arrows themselves were small, hollow "tubes" of cane that were filled with flammable materials. The razor-sharp tip of the arrow would also be dipped in flammable "pitch" and when the archer would pull back the bow, the tip of the arrow would be set afire and released. When this flaming arrow would impact its intended target, the materials inside the cane shaft would splatter in all different directions, setting anything and anyone that was in the vicinity ablaze. This same technique was used with great criticism during the Vietnam war. It was called Napalm.

If any soldier was to be hit with one of these arrows, it certainly meant a horrific death. Any soldier naïve enough to think that he could enter this battle on his own would often perish shortly after entering the battle because the arrows seldom came from a single direction and the solitary soldier's flanks would unwittingly become his demise!

The Spiritual Correlation

First, we need to understand the enemy we are engaged in battle with. Every one of us has heard it said about our sitting president at the time of writing this, "How can you fight an enemy that you cannot name?" Now, I do not want to get into a debate as to whether his approach is the right one. I will not devolve God's word into trite politics, but the application of this is important to us here. The important thing to understand in battling groups like ISIS, Al-Qaeda, Boko Haram, The Islamic Revolutionary Guard (Quds Force), The Haqqani Network, or Hezbollah is the ideology that motivates their actions. If we do not understand the enemy, then we cannot defeat the enemy. The more one knows about his enemy, the more likely he is to be victorious in battle. I am not going to get into too much detail about who our enemy is—you can go back and read chapter 10 "A Call to Arms".

Our enemy is the "Evil One"—a REAL PERSON—not some

The Shield of Faith

abstract idea or philosophy. Our enemy is none other than Satan himself, the Father of Lies, the one who constantly prowls around seeking undefended and weak souls that he may easily seduce and devour.

The Darts or Arrows that we must defend against are quite simply "seducing temptations" offered to elicit ungodly, un-Christ-like, evil behavior in us!

Pay attention to that. We are constantly being bombarded with temptations that are designed to get us to behave and act in an ungodly manner, Un-Christ-like and evil!

It is a list of sins that is entirely too long to fully list here.

Impurity, selfishness, self-sufficiency, pride, doubt, fear, disappointment, lust, greed, vanity, anger, covetousness, the lust of the flesh, the lust of the eyes, the pride of life . . .

> But I say, walk by the Spirit, and you will not gratify the desires of the flesh. For the desires of the flesh are against the Spirit, and the desires of the Spirit are against the flesh, for these are opposed to each other, to keep you from doing the things you want to do. But if you are led by the Spirit, you are not under the law. Now the works of the flesh are evident: sexual immorality, impurity, sensuality, idolatry, sorcery, enmity, strife, jealousy, fits of anger, rivalries, dissensions, divisions, envy, drunkenness, orgies, and things like these. I warn you, as I warned you before, that those who do such things will not inherit the kingdom of God.
>
> Galatians 5:16-21

What then is our "spiritual" Shield of Faith? How does it protect us from those temptations and how do we use and apply it?

Faith—The key word to focus on from this passage in Ephesians is the word "Faith." We are to "Take up the Shield of Faith."

Habakkuk 2:4b " . . . but the righteous shall live by his faith."

Romans 1:17b " . . . the righteous shall live by faith."
Galatians 3:11b " . . . the righteous shall live by faith."

Everybody has faith in something, even professing atheists have a great deal of faith in things that they cannot see, feel, or touch. Faith that when you turn on your faucet that water will come out. Not only that but also that the water that does come out will be clean and potable. Faith that when you get in your car and turn the key, it will start and run reliably enough to get you to where you're going and back. Faith that when you get into an elevator, it will take you to your desired floor and not free fall to the bottom of the shaft and kill everyone. Faith in gravity that when you throw something into the air, it will come back down each and every single time. Faith that the sun will rise again tomorrow, though you may have no idea how that happens.

Lies and Truths

> You are of your father the devil, and your will is to do your father's desires. He was a murderer from the beginning and does not stand in the truth, because there is no truth in him. When he lies, he speaks out of his own character, for he is a liar and the father of lies.
>
> John 8:44

Here again, we see the importance of knowing our enemy. He is a liar and the father of lies—Every flaming arrow we must defend against is another of Satan's lies. If we believe the lie, then we are not believing God who is the ultimate truth. If we know God's truth and firmly and with resolve believe it in faith, then we will not fall victim to the lies of our enemy! The very first arrow fired in this spiritual war was in the Garden of Eden.
God Said:

> And the Lord God commanded the man, saying, "You may surely eat of every tree of the garden, but of the tree

of the knowledge of good and evil you shall not eat, for in the day that you eat of it you shall surely die."
Genesis 2:16-17

When tempted Eve said:

> You shall not eat of the fruit of the tree that is in the midst of the garden, neither shall you touch it, lest you die.
> Genesis 3:3

(Oops—Eve added to God's Word here. God never said touching it would kill her).

Satan said:

> You will not surely die. For God knows that when you eat of it your eyes will be opened, and you will be like God, knowing good and evil.
> Genesis 3:4-5

We all know the story. Eve failed to believe God and fell for Satan's lie. The end result of this lack of faith? 6,000 years of bloody warfare! Every time we fall into sin, we buy into Satan's lies. God tells us don't, Satan stands behind us whispering in our ears, do it, do it, do it! It gets even worse than that. When we fail to believe God, we are making Him out to be a liar which in itself is a lie because God cannot lie!

> Whoever believes in the Son of God has the testimony in himself. Whoever does not believe God has made him a liar, because he has not believed in the testimony that God has borne concerning his Son.
> 1 John 5:10

> ... God, who never lies ...
> Titus 1:2

The Reality of Life

The Bible tells us that, "God will supply all of our needs according to his riches in glory in Christ Jesus." (Philippians 4:19) We say "AMEN." Then we lose a job. We say "Hallelujah." And a spouse leaves. We say "Praise God." And a child's heart fails. An injury cripples us for life. But the truth to be found in God's word tells us that even in the midst of tumult and turmoil that we are blessed.

Psalm 119

> Blessed is the one who reads aloud the words of this prophecy, and blessed are those who hear, and who keep what is written in it, for the time is near.
>
> Revelation 1:3
>
> And we are writing these things so that our joy may be complete.
>
> 1 John 1:4

Abraham believed God and it was counted unto him as Righteousness! So must we believe God! It is then Faith in the truth of God and His Word that enables us to stand against all the flaming arrows of the evil one and to be comforted in these afflictions.

> ...God of all comfort, who comforts us in all our affliction, so that we may be able to comfort those who are in any affliction, with the comfort with which we ourselves are comforted by God.
>
> 2 Corinthians 1:4
>
> Every word of God proves true; he is a shield to those who take refuge in him.
>
> Proverbs 30:5

The Shield of Faith

> "Because the poor are plundered, because the needy groan, I will now arise," says the Lord; "I will place him in the safety for which he longs." The words of the Lord are pure words, like silver refined in a furnace on the ground, purified seven times. You, O Lord, will keep them; you will guard us from this generation forever. On every side the wicked prowl, as vileness is exalted among the children of man.
>
> Psalm 12:5-8

> This God—his way is perfect; the word of the Lord proves true; he is a shield for all those who take refuge in him.
>
> Psalm 18:30

Resist the temptations of your mortal enemy in steadfast faith . . . The Lord of Hosts is a mighty tower that we can run into and be safe!

> Humble yourselves, therefore, under the mighty hand of God so that at the proper time he may exalt you, casting all your anxieties on him, because he cares for you. Be sober-minded; be watchful. Your adversary the devil prowls around like a roaring lion, seeking someone to devour. Resist him, firm in your faith, knowing that the same kinds of suffering are being experienced by your brotherhood throughout the world.
>
> 1 Peter 5:8-9

> God is our refuge and strength, a very present help in trouble. Therefore, we will not fear though the earth gives way, though the mountains be moved into the heart of the sea, though its waters roar and foam, though the mountains tremble at its swelling. Selah There is a river whose streams make glad the city of God, the holy

habitation of the Most High. God is in the midst of her; she shall not be moved; God will help her when morning dawns. The nations rage, the kingdoms totter; he utters his voice, the earth melts. The Lord of hosts is with us; the God of Jacob is our fortress. Selah Come, behold the works of the Lord, how he has brought desolations on the earth. He makes wars cease to the end of the earth; he breaks the bow and shatters the spear; he burns the chariots with fire. "Be still and know that I am God. I will be exalted among the nations, I will be exalted in the earth!" The Lord of hosts is with us; the God of Jacob is our fortress. Selah

Psalm 46

How lovely is your dwelling place, O Lord of hosts! My soul longs, yes, faints for the courts of the Lord; my heart and flesh sing for joy to the living God. Even the sparrow finds a home, and the swallow a nest for herself, where she may lay her young, at your altars, O Lord of hosts, my King and my God. Blessed are those who dwell in your house, ever singing your praise! Selah Blessed are those whose strength is in you, in whose heart are the highways to Zion. As they go through the Valley of Baca, they make it a place of springs; the early rain also covers it with pools. They go from strength to strength; each one appears before God in Zion. O Lord God of hosts, hear my prayer; give ear, O God of Jacob! Selah Behold our shield, O God; look on the face of your anointed! For a day in your courts is better than a thousand elsewhere. I would rather be a doorkeeper in the house of my God than dwell in the tents of wickedness. For the Lord God is a sun and shield; the Lord bestows favor and honor. No good thing does he withhold from those who walk uprightly. O Lord of hosts blessed is the one who trusts in you!

The Shield of Faith

Psalm 84

The name of the Lord is a strong tower; the righteous man runs into it and is safe.

Proverbs 18:10

Holding the Shield of Faith and "standing" against the attacks of the enemy boils down to one simple concept. It is the consistent application of what we know about God to the daily issues of our lives and then trusting Him in that truth. If we do not trust God fully in every situation, then it is obvious that we do not know Him well enough yet! Remember that the victory in this battle has already been won!

What then shall we say to these things? If God is for us, who can be against us? He who did not spare his own Son but gave him up for us all, how will he not also with him graciously give us all things? Who shall bring any charge against God's elect? It is God who justifies. Who is to condemn? Christ Jesus is the one who died—more than that, who was raised—who is at the right hand of God, who indeed is interceding for us. Who shall separate us from the love of Christ? Shall tribulation, or distress, or persecution, or famine, or nakedness, or danger, or sword? As it is written, "For your sake we are being killed all day long; we are regarded as sheep to be slaughtered." No, in all these things we are more than conquerors through him who loved us. For I am sure that neither death nor life, nor angels nor rulers, nor things present nor things to come, nor powers, nor height nor depth, nor anything else in all creation, will be able to separate us from the love of God in Christ Jesus our Lord.

Romans 8:31-39

The Christ in my Cancer

We are "super" conquerors in Christ Jesus!

> And when they began to sing and praise, the Lord set an ambush against the men of Ammon, Moab, and Mount Seir, who had come against Judah, so that they were routed. For the men of Ammon and Moab rose against the inhabitants of Mount Seir, devoting them to destruction, and when they had made an end of the inhabitants of Seir, they all helped to destroy one another.
>
> 2 Chronicles 20:22-23

This is probably the best passage to remember as the battle gets heavy! When the people of God began to praise Him and worship Him, God set an ambush against their enemies! Their enemies began to fight amongst themselves, killing each other off before God's people even enter the fight! God's people were given all of the spoils to keep as their own! Every other people group feared them as they celebrated God's victory!

It is important to note again, God had done all the fighting and once He had won the battle, He gave all of the spoils and riches to his people! He has promised to do the same for us if we remain faithful to His truth. He will fight the fight for us so that we never have to lift a hand to our enemy! God will give us all of the spoils! How then is this victory won in the daily battle against sin and temptation?

Praise and worship God at all times and in all things, regardless of what we seem to think of our present situation. God can overcome it FOR US! When Satan tempts you with a lie, find the contradictory truth in Scripture and stand firm in it! Commit yourself to know His word inside and out. Your eternal survival may just depend on it. Be holy as He is holy and remains confident that in Christ Jesus you will be victorious, that in Christ Jesus who strengthens you, you can defeat all of the schemes of the evil one!

When the affairs and temptations of this life begin to wear you down and defeat you, do not let your emotions take hold, bringing

The Shield of Faith

you down in defeat and discouragement. Take hold instead of the great promises of God and cling to what the Word of God says. Do not live by your circumstances but instead choose to live by faith. Confidence and trust in God that He will do exactly as He promises to do. I have no idea what the future holds for me regarding my brain cancer diagnosis, but I am content (most days) that He has it all under control and that He will be glorified in it.

The holding up of the shield of faith reminds us that we are dependent on God and His Grace in Jesus Christ who has all power and who will enable us to be more than conquerors! And finally, remember that this shield we carry can defeat ALL of the flaming arrows of the evil one. Not some. Not most. ALL. Every single one without exception! Every attack, every ambush, every arrow is extinguished by this shield! This shield is most effective when it is used in combination with others! We are not on this battlefield alone. We MUST come together as the army of God and stand together, protecting the "body" with the tortoise shell of protection provided by our shields held together against the enemy.

In this remember, if you drop your shield, it is not only yourself that you put at risk, it is also your brother/sister sitting next to you that you are putting at risk since your shield cannot be added to the "tortoise shell" and its absence leaves a gaping hole where arrows can penetrate!

CHAPTER 15

The Helmet of Salvation

"Family" Prayer

Pray for each other without knowing what exactly the need is. Those with a need should raise their hands but not state what the need is, and those who do not should go to their brother or sister and pray for them without knowing the need. Pray for God's will in their lives, that God would be honored in their need, that God would provide His strength in their need, that the Holy Spirit would provide comfort and wisdom, and that even during the storm they would be given peace.

Change of Urgency

Most times I do not want to be giving the messages that I do, because I realize that many times these messages cut and cut deeply. I truly do not wish to cause pain for anybody. It breaks my heart to hurt. I do not want to generate the feeling that I know some messages do, but I am faced with a choice. I could preach sermons that leave people feeling good about themselves, sermons without any conviction or pain, but then, that would provide no more benefit to the listeners than a night at the movies or the concert of a favorite band. Beyond that even, am I honoring God should I bring messages that have no conviction or biblical truth in them? I will after all answer to Him one day for what I say when standing behind this making these statements!

These messages, and many like them, are intended to cut.

The Christ in my Cancer

Sometimes they are intended to cut deeply. I know that going in, and never relish the idea of giving them, but if you had cancer—as I now do—would you not want someone who was skilled with a knife to cut as deeply as necessary to remove it? Would you not be willing to deal with whatever pain was necessary for the removal of cancer? Would you be willing to wait 2 years for surgery because putting it off is less painful than dealing with it now?

To that end is the intent behind these messages. To find the cancer of sin and misinformation that is destroying us and remove it—to cut it out immediately and completely at whatever cost, because failure to do so means that this cancer of sin will consume us and lead to our imminent deaths.

> Finally, be strong in the Lord and in the strength of his might. Put on the whole armor of God, that you may be able to stand against the schemes of the devil. For we do not wrestle against flesh and blood, but against the rulers, against the authorities, against the cosmic powers over this present darkness, against the spiritual forces of evil in the heavenly places. Therefore take up the whole armor of God, that you may be able to withstand in the evil day, and having done all, to stand firm. Stand therefore, having fastened on the belt of truth, and having put on the breastplate of righteousness, and, as shoes for your feet, having put on the readiness given by the gospel of peace. In all circumstances take up the shield of faith, with which you can extinguish all the flaming darts of the evil one; and take the helmet of salvation, and the sword of the Spirit, which is the word of God, praying at all times in the Spirit, with all prayer and supplication. To that end keep alert with all perseverance, making supplication for all the saints, and also for me, that words may be given to me in opening my mouth boldly to proclaim the mystery of the gospel.
>
> Ephesians 6:10-19

The Helmet of Salvation

Are there any influences on your life that should not be there? Influences that do not honor God.

Influences that are clearly wicked in nature if not in action? Influences that depict anti-Christ as the reluctant hero.

(Are most of us ready to answer "no" to that question?) The obvious ones should be easy. You are probably not engaging in witchcraft. You are likely not using a Ouija board. You should not be engaged in adultery or prostitution. I don't think you are associating with gangsters or murderers. By the way, if you ARE engaged in any of these activities, SHAME ON YOU—STOP IT AND STOP IT NOW!

The subtle ones are not so obvious. Do you watch shows which depict the afterlife as a war between those who are "alive" and demonic mindless zombies? What kind of music do you listen to? Did you mourn and grieve when hedonistic, secular musicians die? Do you watch shows that are rife with improper conduct and sensual acts? Do you entertain media that elevates the occult? Are you a fan of media that depicts reluctant heroes, usually with supernatural powers, who have to give their own lives to save all of humanity?

What about the idols of holidays that are reserved for Christ alone/? Where Jesus Christ, the ONLY Son of God who gave His life for ours, is reduced to cheap slogans on the front of our churches and little plastic eggs filled with candy? How about the guy who, at the end of the year, teaches our children that if only they have done enough "good works" throughout the year, they can reap the reward due them because of their "goodness" and gain blessings in the form of the things they want while avoiding the punishment of receiving "coal"?

Are there any areas of your life where you have accepted the lifestyle of the wicked and adopted it as your own? How do you view a couple who is living together outside of marriage? How about gender-neutral bathrooms? Homosexual marriage? Practicing homosexuals in ministry? How about your speech? Do you allow, accept, and even use profanity? Do you use or tolerate speech outside of the church that you would NEVER allow inside of the church? Do you participate in or just sit idly by while sexually or racially inappropriate conversations take place, or do you remove yourself or even speak up about the inappropriate nature of the conversation?

Do you sit idly by while your Savior is blasphemed, or do you rise to His defense even though it might mean you won't be invited to the next neighborhood block party? What about your clothing? Do you (especially you, ladies) wear clothing that is respectable or can your attire be considered salacious at times? Do you "sit in the seat of scoffers"? Do you insist that others live under a law that God never gave such as those who insist that the King James version of the Bible is the only one that is acceptable?

Or do you "delight in the law of the Lord"? When you read God's word do you find passages of Scripture that validate the beliefs you bring to the table or are you earnestly searching for God's truth, allowing IT to mold and modify your beliefs? Does the "Law of the Lord" (His word) somehow cramp your style? Are there areas in your life that you are simply unwilling to surrender to Him? If God were to give you a "Get out of jail Free" card, which of his laws, would you choose to break? Would it be adultery? How about lying, drunkenness, or murder? Which of God's laws would you really like permission to break? If we truly do "delight in the law of the Lord," we can prove it by putting on the Helmet of Salvation and meditating on His word "day and night."

What does it mean, then, to meditate on the law of God both day and night? It means that God's word, His plan of Salvation, should be the "chief occupation of our minds" and central to our lives! We should study it, think about it, consider it and apply it as effortlessly as we breathe or as reliably as our hearts pump life-giving blood throughout our veins without a conscious effort on our part. It must become "instinctive" rather than "intentional" and for that to become reality it takes effort on our part! It is not about talent, intelligence, or education.

It starts with an understanding of the necessity of the knowledge and understanding of God's Word and eventually leads to an obsession with it! Discipline eventually turns into delight! As we spend more and more time studying and applying His Word we will eventually become "Like trees planted by streams of water" that "yield our fruits in their season" and our "leaves will never wither!"

Take The Helmet of Salvation

First, we must start with an understanding of what exactly the "Bible" is. It is God's Holy word, of course. His instruction manual for how we are to live our lives and a battle manual for the warfare that we are engaged in.

But what God's word is first and foremost is, in its entirety, a complete and detailed plan for God's salvation of His fallen creation. Every word, from Genesis 1:1 through to Revelation 22:21, is the story of God's grace in action, His work of redeeming sinful mankind, and His work of salvation.

The salvation of the Messiah is here represented as a helmet, covering the head, for the warrior does not hide or cower behind his shield, but looks over the top of it into the face of his opponent.

That which adorns and protects the Christian Warrior, and which enables us to hold our heads above the shield with confidence and joy, is the fact that we are and will be saved.

What was the helmet that Paul was referring to here as worn by the Roman soldiers of the time? The helmet is a vital piece of armor for the warrior on the battlefield as a blow to the head is almost always fatal. It is used to protect "the mind" (the center of thinking) of the wearer. It was made of a very tough metal like iron to defend against a blow from a two-handed broad sword. It had a lining inside of leather or felt to provide padding against a blow. It covered not only the head but also covered the back of the neck and the shoulder area. On top, it generally had a colorful plume that not only identified the army for which the wearer fought but also was an inspiration to others who were following into the battle. But Paul tells us specifically that this piece of armor is the helmet "of Salvation."

What exactly does that mean? Aren't we already saved and no longer need to consider it? In one respect, yes. We have already received the gift of salvation through Christ when His work was completed at the cross. We have been JUSTIFIED in Christ.

> There is therefore now no condemnation for those who are in Christ Jesus. For the law of the Spirit of life has set you free in Christ Jesus from the law of sin and death. For God has done what the law, weakened by the flesh, could not do. By sending his own Son in the likeness of sinful flesh and for sin, he condemned sin in the flesh, in order that the righteous requirement of the law might be fulfilled in us, who walk not according to the flesh but according to the Spirit.
>
> Romans 8:1-4

In another sense, though we are still in the process of being saved. This is the SANCTIFICATION that all disciples of Christ experience through the Holy Spirit.

> But when the goodness and loving kindness of God our Savior appeared, He saved us, not because of works done by us in righteousness, but according to His own mercy, by the washing of regeneration and renewal of the Holy Spirit, whom he poured out on us richly through Jesus Christ our Savior, so that being justified by his grace we might become heirs according to the hope of eternal life.
>
> Titus 3:4-7

> As you come to him, a living stone rejected by men but in the sight of God chosen and precious, you yourselves like living stones are being built up as a spiritual house, to be a holy priesthood, to offer spiritual sacrifices acceptable to God through Jesus Christ.
>
> 1 Peter 2:4-5

The Helmet of Salvation

Here we clearly see that we have already been justified in Christ but are also being "regenerated and renewed" by the Holy Spirit. "As we come to Him" in His word, we will be "Built Up" to be His holy priesthood! This is sanctification!

In a third sense, we will also be saved in the future once we stand with Him in eternity. This is GLORIFICATION.

> And those whom he predestined he also called, and those whom he called he also justified, and those whom he justified he also glorified.
>
> Romans 8:30

The helmet that we wear is not only the assurance of our justification and the evidence of our sanctification, but it is also the hope of our glorification.

> But since we belong to the day, let us be sober, having put on the breastplate of faith and love, and for a helmet the hope of salvation.
>
> 1 Thessalonians 5:8

> "But the one who endures to the end will be saved."
>
> Matthew 24:13

> And you, who once were alienated and hostile in mind, doing evil deeds, He has now reconciled in his body of flesh by His death, in order to present you holy and blameless and above reproach before Him, if indeed you continue in the faith, stable and steadfast, not shifting from the hope of the gospel that you heard, which has been proclaimed in all creation under heaven, and of which I, Paul, became a minister.
>
> Colossians 1:21-23

Continue in the Faith

> "Abide in me, and I in you. As the branch cannot bear fruit by itself, unless it abides in the vine, neither can you, unless you abide in Me.'"
>
> John 15:4

Stable and Steadfast

> rooted and built up in Him and established in the faith, just as you were taught, abounding in thanksgiving.
>
> Colossians 2:7

> so that Christ may dwell in your hearts through faith—that you, being rooted and grounded in love.
>
> Ephesians 3:17

In properly adorning the "Helmet of Salvation" we should understand that we are to (through the study and application of God's Word) develop the "Mind of Christ".

> Finally, brothers, whatever is true, whatever is honorable, whatever is just, whatever is pure, whatever is lovely, whatever is commendable, if there is any excellence, if there is anything worthy of praise, think about these things. What you have learned and received and heard and seen in me—practice these things, and the God of peace will be with you.
>
> Philippians 4:8-9

> For those who live according to the flesh set their minds on the things of the flesh, but those who live according to the Spirit set their minds on the things of the Spirit.
>
> Romans 8:5

The Helmet of Salvation

So, flee youthful passions and pursue righteousness, faith, love, and peace, along with those who call on the Lord from a pure heart. Have nothing to do with foolish, ignorant controversies; you know that they breed quarrels.

2 Timothy 2:22-23

The head is extremely vulnerable in this spiritual battle in which we are engaged. If we believe that we can "lose" our salvation, then we will be ill-equipped to battle with the enemy of our Lord. The mind is the birthplace of our emotions. Our emotions are "fickle" and "sinful". These emotions are at the root of spiritual deception and doubt.

The Helmet of Salvation, therefore, protects us from doubt, discouragement, dread, and fear. The Helmet is our Hope of Salvation and gives us confidence in the face of our foe.

The Hope of Salvation in Christ, protected and sustained by the helmet, is the rock that anchors us and assures us that, in Christ, we have not only experienced victory over our enemy but will also continue to stand against him until the end of this battle.

in hope of eternal life, which God, who never lies, promised before the ages began

Titus 1:2

And we desire each one of you to show the same earnestness to have the full assurance of hope until the end, so that you may not be sluggish, but imitators of those who through faith and patience inherit the promises.

Hebrews 6:11-12

Preach "The Gospel" to yourself daily and often multiple times throughout the day!

When you realize that you are a sinner, remember the cross of Christ and what He accomplished for you there. It is not about what you do for Him, but it is about what He did for you at Calvary! When you are weak, broken, or scared, remember that you can do all things through Christ who strengthens you! When you feel worthless, remember that it is no longer you who live, but Christ who lives in you, you are worth more even than the very life of God's own Son! When you feel alone and unloved, remember the love that God showed you when He gave His only begotten Son so that you would not perish! When you grow weary of the battle, remember that you are commanded to stand and when you have given it everything you have, to stand even more! When your life is crumbling around you, remember that He is the rock upon which your foundation is laid, and in Him, you can find refuge! When life overwhelms you and you feel that you can't go on, turn to Jesus Christ, take His yoke upon you and He will give you rest! When all you want to do is to give up the fight and find somewhere where there is peace, remember that you have not yet begun to see, hear or imagine what God has planned for you. Remember that you are no longer your own, but that you have been bought and paid for at an unimaginable price. Nothing less than the spilled blood of God's own Son mingling and mixing on the ground with the dust of His own creation! Stay in His word daily so that you may be able to "withstand all the flaming darts of the evil one"! Remember that we were once all "wolves" and through the cross of Christ, God takes us and transforms us into His sheep by removing our heart of stone and replacing it with a heart of flesh after His own making and He places us under His constant and tender care! Remember that NOTHING can separate you from the love of God in Jesus Christ! Remain confident that while the battle rages on, the war is won and we are already victorious in Christ!

Think about the end of WWII—the Japanese had surrendered, yet the fighting continued on many remote islands for years to come. The war was over, but there were still places where we could not walk with abandon and carelessness!

And above all else, when the storm of life is raging, remember that He is the one who stills the water and calms the seas. He is the one who, right now at this very moment, is standing with you, protecting

The Helmet of Salvation

and keeping you as His own, and has promised to never leave you or forsake you!

Paul Washer preached a message about the blessing for those in a covenant relationship with God through faith in Jesus. Instruction in the word leads to obedience and it marks their lives with love, joy, peace, and fruitfulness in their character. Does that describe you?

It's either yes or no. Does it? Is your life marked by peace, love, joy, and fruitfulness, or are you sad, lonely, miserable, and constantly complaining about your "lot in life"? Have you entered into a covenant relationship with God? Strictly speaking, a covenant is an unchangeable, divinely imposed, legal agreement between God and man that stipulates the conditions of the relationship.

Divinely imposed means that we have absolutely no negotiation regarding the covenant. It is a covenant defined by God and we can only accept the covenant or reject it!

A covenant relationship was serious business in ancient times. It was the strongest and most solemn bondmen could make and was often solemnized through great ceremony and ritual.

The triune Godhead has such a covenant relationship regarding us.

God the Father has covenanted (promised) to count our sins against God the Son and in return count His righteousness towards us.

God the Son has covenanted (promised) to die in our place and take our sins upon Himself.

God the Spirit has covenanted (promised) to never leave us or forsake us and to hold us and keep us, sanctifying us for the Son. God has defined a covenantal relationship between Himself and mankind as well.

> Therefore He (Jesus Christ) is the mediator of a new covenant, so that those who are called may receive the promised eternal inheritance, since a death has occurred that redeems them from the transgressions committed under the first covenant.
>
> Hebrews 9:15

The Christ in my Cancer

So then, have you entered into a covenant relationship with God? Yes, or no? Have you? Do you violently cling to His Son as your ONLY hope of salvation? DO YOU? Are you PERSONALLY and CONSISTENTLY being instructed by the Holy Spirit in His Word? Are You? Do you consciously and submissively walk according to His Word? DO YOU? Do you exhibit the "Real Peace" that transcends all understanding? Have you SAVORED the fact that you now have peace with God? Do you have that peace during the turmoil of your life? Have you grown in His word until you can experience this peace? Do you have hope? Do you hope for more than this life has to offer or are you sadly content with the things of this world?

Are you intentionally and purposely fruitful? Do you PASSIONATELY desire to produce more fruit for Him? And finally, are you conscious of your blessed state in Him?

> The LORD is my shepherd; I shall not want. He makes me lie down in green pastures. He leads me beside still waters. He restores my soul. He leads me in paths of righteousness for his name's sake. Even though I walk through the valley of the shadow of death, I will fear no evil, for you are with me; your rod and your staff, they comfort me. You prepare a table before me in the presence of my enemies; you anoint my head with oil; my cup overflows. Surely goodness and mercy shall follow me all the days of my life, and I shall dwell in the house of the LORD forever.
>
> Psalm 23

In short, when we wear and apply the "Helmet of Salvation," we are living out the words of the hymn "Trust and Obey" written in 1919 by James Sammis.

The Helmet of Salvation

The song goes like this:

> When we walk with the Lord in the light of his
> Word, what a glory he sheds on our way!
> While we do his good will, he abides with us still,
> and with all who will trust and obey.
> Trust and obey, for there's no other way to be happy
> in Jesus, but to trust and obey.
> Not a shadow can rise, not a cloud in the skies, but
> his smile quickly drives it away.
> Not a doubt or a fear, not a sigh nor a tear, can abide
> while we trust and obey.
> Trust and obey, for there's no other way to be happy
> in Jesus, but to trust and obey.
> Not a burden we bear, not a sorrow we share, but
> our toil he doth richly repay.
> Not a grief nor a loss, not a frown or a cross, but is
> blest if we trust and obey.
> Trust and obey, for there's no other way to be happy
> in Jesus, but to trust and obey.
> But we never can prove the delights of his love until
> all on the altar we lay.
> For the favor he shows, and the joy he bestows, are
> for them who will trust and obey.
> Trust and obey, for there's no other way to be happy
> in Jesus, but to trust and obey.
> Then in fellowship sweet we will sit at his feet, or
> we'll walk by his side in the way.
> What he says we will do, where he sends, we will go,
> never fear, only trust, and obey.

CHAPTER 16

The Sword of the Spirit

The Best Defense is a Good Offense

Finally, be strong in the Lord and in the strength of his might. Put on the whole armor of God, that you may be able to stand against the schemes of the devil. For we do not wrestle against flesh and blood, but against the rulers, against the authorities, against the cosmic powers over this present darkness, against the spiritual forces of evil in the heavenly places. Therefore, take up the whole armor of God, that you may be able to withstand in the evil day, and having done all, to stand firm. Stand therefore, having fastened on the belt of truth, and having put on the breastplate of righteousness, and, as shoes for your feet, having put on the readiness given by the gospel of peace. In all circumstances take up the shield of faith, with which you can extinguish all the flaming darts of the evil one; and take the helmet of salvation, and the sword of the Spirit, which is the word of God, always praying in the Spirit, with all prayer and supplication. To that end keep alert with all perseverance, making supplication for all the saints, and for me, that words may be given to me in opening my mouth boldly to proclaim the mystery of the gospel.

Ephesians 6:10-19

The Christ in my Cancer

Historical Context

No army has ever won a war through a defensive strategy alone. Victory can only be achieved through the proper use of both defensive AND offensive measures. A defensive-only strategy does not provide for victory. It only serves to postpone defeat!

When we think of a sword, we typically think of the "Two-Handed Broad Sword." but just as we do today, the Romans had one word that described several different things within a classification.

If I were to tell you I had a knife in my pocket, you would naturally think of a "Pocket knife" or as my grandfather used to call it, a "Pen Knife." But what about a "Butter Knife" or a "Fillet Knife"?

The word used in Greek for this knife was "machairan" which, when properly translated shows us that this particular "Sword" was more of a knife to our point of reference than a sword.

It was typically between 12 and 18 inches in length, was approximately 2 Inches across, and was sharpened on both sides. It was more like today's "Marine K-Bar" than it was what we typically think of as a sword.

It was composed of a metal blade, which was usually bronze or iron in the biblical period, and a wood or bone handle. Since swords were so common in the ancient world, the biblical writers provided few descriptive details about these weapons.

> And Ehud made for himself a sword with two edges, a cubit in length, and he bound it on his right thigh under his clothes. And he presented the tribute to Eglon king of Moab. Now Eglon was a very fat man. And when Ehud had finished presenting the tribute, he sent away the people who carried the tribute. But he turned back at the idols near Gilgal and said, I have a secret message for you, O king. And he commanded, Silence. And all his attendants went out from his presence. And Ehud came to him as he was sitting alone in his cool roof chamber. And Ehud said, I have a message from God for you. And

The Sword of the Spirit

he arose from his seat. And Ehud reached with his left hand, took the sword from his right thigh, and thrust it into his belly. And the hilt also went in after the blade, and the fat closed over the blade, for he did not pull the sword out of his belly; and the dung came out.

Judges 3:16-22

It was an up-close and personal weapon, designed to be used in very close hand-to-hand combat with surgical precision, often being thrust through the ribcage, deep into the chest of the opponent, and directly into the heart. The result of this attack often caused immediate death.

Take up the Sword of the Spirit

The Enemy

Our enemy is the "Father of lies." How can we ever negotiate with a consummate liar?

There is no reference in this passage to talk, negotiate or compromise. The order is given—"Take the Sword."

Understanding this passage accepts as a conclusion the following.

There is to be no compromise with the enemy. There shall be no treaty of peace with our enemy. We are to give the enemy no quarter in this battle. We are not to negotiate with the enemy of God. There are no orders from our Captain to "patch up a truce."

The world would have us compromise for the sake of "peace," but understand that this "worldly peace" is spiritual death to us. THERE CAN BE NO TRUE PEACE UNTIL EVERY KNEE HAS BOWED before the creator of all existence!

The Sword is an "offensive" weapon. We are to not only defend but also to assail with it! IT IS NOT ENOUGH THAT WE SIMPLY "NOT BE CONQUERED." WE MUST ALSO CONQUER! We are not told to "Take up the Spear" and fight from a distance, vanquishing our enemy with sterile anonymity, but are commanded to "Take up the

Sword" and engage God's enemy in the very midst of the bloodshed and carnage. In other words, we are going to get bloody in this battle! Remember that this enemy does not lie afar, off at a distance, but lies as close as our very own hearts, hiding deep within the wilderness of the sin in our lives and we must use surgical precision with this sword and thrust it deep within the heart to route the destroyer of our souls.

The Sword:

Our sword is the word of God. And what a weapon it is!

> For the word of God is living and active, sharper than any two-edged sword, piercing to the division of soul and of spirit, of joints and of marrow, and discerning the thoughts and intentions of the heart.
>
> Hebrews 4:12

It is a 2-edged sword. The first is God's love and the other, opposing edge, is God's wrath!

I have heard it said by many that we are to "love the lost into Heaven." Others have told me that we should "scare them out of Hell." Either practiced singularly would only make use of half of the sword. Half of God's divine word. Did not God give us ALL of His word? Was it not ALL INSPIRED of the Holy Spirit? Who then are we to say that love alone or fear alone is the tactic to be practiced? What audacity that we would presume of God that he would have us use only a portion of what he has given us for this battle!

> The Lord is a lord of war; the Lord is his name.
>
> Exodus 15:3

> Anyone who does not love does not know God, because God is love.
>
> 1 John 4:8

The Sword of the Spirit

Our Sword though is not the entirety of God's word as would be the case if the word used here was "Logos", but it is not. The word used for sword in this passage is "Rhema" which essentially refers to specific passages within the "Logos".

We must become adept at applying the specifics of God's word to the specific temptation we face. If we don't know what God has to say about our specific situation then how will we be able to deal with it as God desires?

Our Sword is Complete—It contains everything we need

Excerpt from John Wesley sermon *The Bible is an Armory*:
"The Bible could ONLY have been written by:
Good Men or Good Angels—But they could not have, because the Bible does not give these men and angels the credit for authorship. Who would write such a book and give complete credit to another?
Bad Men or Bad Angels—But this could not be the case, because the Bible condemns both these Bad Men and Bad Angels. Who would write a book that condemns themselves?
God—Divine Authorship alone then would be the only remaining possibility. We, then, had better pay attention to the words within and heed what they must tell us!
Guthrie – "The Bible is an Armory of Heavenly Weapons"
It is a laboratory of infallible medicine... It is a mine of exhaustive wealth... It is a guidebook for every road... It is a chart for every sea... It is medicine for every malady... It is balm for every wound... [16]"

The Bible contains History, Genealogy, Ethnicity, Law, Ethics, Poetry, Prophecy, Eloquence, Medicine, Politics, Economics, Sanitary Guidelines, Science, Etc.

16 Guthrie, T, *The Bible is an Armory*. Sermon Central.https://www.sermoncentral.com/sermon-illustrations/62528/thomas-guthrie-said-the-bible-is-an-armory-of-by-gene-gregory Viewed October 11, 2022

In its whole, the Word is Infallible

The law of the Lord is perfect.

Psalm 19:7a

In its parts, the Word is Inerrant.

Every word of God proves true; he is a shield to those who take refuge in him.

Proverbs 30:5a

The Word is Complete.

I warn everyone who hears the words of the prophecy of this book: if anyone adds to them, God will add to him the plagues described in this book, and if anyone takes away from the words of the book of this prophecy, God will take away his share in the tree of life and in the holy city, which are described in this book.

Revelation 22:18,19

The Word is Authoritative

Hear, O heavens, and give ear, O earth; for the Lord has spoken

Isaiah 1:2a

The Word is Sufficient

All Scripture is breathed out by God and profitable for teaching, for reproof, for correction, and for training in righteousness, that the man of God may be complete, equipped for every good work.

2 Timothy 3:16,17

The Sword of the Spirit

The Word is Effective

"So shall my word be that goes out from my mouth; it shall not return to me empty, but it shall accomplish that which I purpose, and shall succeed in the thing for which I sent it."

Isaiah 55:11

The Word is of Divine Nature

For no prophecy was ever produced by the will of man, but men spoke from God as they were carried along by the Holy Spirit.

2 Peter 1:21

The Word is Determinative

Our attitude towards it is an indication of our eternal status.

"Whoever is of God hears the words of God. The reason why you do not hear them is that you are not of God."

John 8:47

The Word is the source of Truth

"Sanctify them in the truth; your word is truth" It is the truth regarding Life, Death, Time, Eternity, Heaven, Hell, Right, Wrong, Men, Women, Society, Relationships . . .

John 17:17

The Word is the Source of Happiness

"Blessed rather are those who hear the word of God and keep it!"

Luke 11:28

The Word is the Source of Power

> Your word is a lamp to my feet and a light to my path.
>
> Psalm 119:105

The Word is the Source of Comfort

> For whatever was written in former days was written for our instruction, that through endurance and through the encouragement of the Scriptures we might have hope.
>
> Romans 15:4

The Word is the Source of Perfection

> All Scripture is breathed out by God and profitable for teaching, for reproof, for correction, and for training in righteousness.
>
> 2 Timothy 3:16

The Word is the Source of Victory

> Take up the Sword of the Spirit
>
> Ephesians 6:17

The Word is sufficient for Training

For the sword to have an edge—any edge at all—It must be possessed of the Holy Spirit and wielded by a warrior who is perfectly trained in its use otherwise it is of no more use than an old almanac. Extensive training is required to effectively use this sword, for who would give this razor-sharp weapon to an infant to wield lest he causes himself harm in the ignorance of its use? Pray that we never think ourselves skilled enough in its use that we require no additional training. Nay, without ongoing training the skills that we have gained will themselves wither and fall away as easily as the details of distant memories from days long since passed.

The Sword of the Spirit

This is the reason that I preach the things we do Sunday after Sunday, systematically through Scripture. It is to help you to know, understand, and become experts in the use of the tools which God has placed at your disposal.

Instructions and Resources

God gives us the details on how we are to live our lives in Ephesians.

In Chapters 4, 5, & 6, He gives us the resources we are to use in Ephesians 1, 2 & 3. Jesus Himself, our Commander in Chief, has given us prime examples of the swords used while He was being tempted by the enemy in the wilderness. He applied the specifics of Scripture to the specific temptation and was therefore victorious against the best that Satan had to offer. We too can have this same victory if only we study to show ourselves approved in the use of God's word.

Satan's first temptation to Jesus:

> If you are the Son of God, command these stones to become loaves of bread.
>
> Matthew 4:3

Jesus' Response:

> But he answered, "It is written, Man shall not live by bread alone, but by every word that comes from the mouth of God."
>
> Matthew 4:4

Satan's second temptation to Jesus:

> "If you are the Son of God, throw yourself down, for it is written, He will command his angels concerning you, and On their hands, they will bear you up, lest you strike your foot against a stone."
>
> Matthew 4:6

Jesus' Response:

> "Again it is written, You shall not put the Lord your God to the test"
>
> Matthew 4:7

Satan's third temptation to Jesus:

> Again, the devil took him to a very high mountain and showed him all the kingdoms of the world and their glory. And he said to him, All these I will give you, if you will fall down and worship me.
>
> Matthew 4:8,9

Jesus' Response:

> "Be gone, Satan! For it is written, 'You shall worship the Lord your God and him only shall you serve."
>
> Matthew 4:10

And in properly wielding the Sword of the Spirit, Jesus gained victory over the Devil.

> Then the devil left him, and behold, angels came and were ministering to him.
>
> Matthew 4:11

Notice each time that Jesus began his counter-attack with "It is Written." Notice also that Jesus did not respond to these temptations with just any passage of Scripture, but with ones that were in direct response to Satan's attack and the result was the enemy fleeing from Him!

The Sword of the Spirit

The Holy Spirit:

The Holy Spirit brings to the forefront of our minds specific passages of Scripture according to the unique battles in which we find ourselves as He draws upon what we have read and learned from our study of God's word!

The Holy Spirit gives us the word as it is needed. The Holy Spirit interprets the word for us. The Holy Spirit teaches us how to use the word effectively.

> Resist the Devil and he will flee from you.
>
> James 4:7

So, how are we to resist?

I have heard it said that we should "Repel the Devil in Jesus' name." Like the name 'Jesus' alone has some sort of magical power that we can lay hold of in our time of need. Isn't that kind of like praying that you will do anything for God if He only gets you out of your present situation?

Was this how Jesus responded in the wilderness? Did he make empty promises to God in Gethsemane if God would get him out of death on the cross? Did Jesus respond to the Devil's temptations by chanting "Get thee away from me Satan in My Own Name!" Now, that's just ridiculous!

No. We resist the Devil the very same way that Jesus did in the wilderness—with the specific application of Scripture that best counters the temptations we are facing!

Understand and be Sanguine in this—the word of God is a weapon and there should be no question regarding this truth. The only hindrance in its use is the skill of the one who wields it, namely you and me!

Study to show yourselves approved. Be in the word at all times! "Faith comes by hearing and hearing by the Word of God." Be in the word at all times! Remember... In its whole, the word is Infallible. In its parts the word is Inerrant. The word is Complete. The word is

Authoritative. The word is Sufficient. The word is Effective.

The word is of Divine Nature. The word is Determinative, i.e. our attitude towards it is an indication of our eternal status. The word is the source of Truth. The word is the source of Happiness. The word is the Source of Power. The word is the source of Comfort.

The word is the source of Perfection. The word is the source of Victory.

This knowledge and knowledge of the words that are in Scripture are not enough though. Knowing how to use a sword does not make one effective on the battlefield. A soldier must have confidence in his weapons if he is to be victorious. He must have faith that it will perform for him as designed every time as he charges headlong into the fight!

We must have more than just an intellectual knowledge of Scripture. For us to be able to wield it effectively, we must: Believe it! Trust it! Hold onto it as if our lives depended upon it!

> Now when they heard this they were cut to the heart
>
> Acts 2:37

When Peter had finished preaching his incredible Gospel message in Acts Chapter 2, we read that the listeners were "Pierced to the Heart" by it.

The Sword of the Spirit delivers a mortal wound directly to the heart that drives us to the emergency room of God's grace and mercy. Just like a surgeon's knife, we must be cut by the scalpel of God's holy word to be healed of the disease of sin that has condemned us to death.

For us to be willing to sign up for the heart transplant that God has promised us, we must first come face to face with the realization that this heart we currently have has been mortally wounded, pierced by the conviction of sin as administered by the sword of the Spirit.

Who in their right mind would volunteer for a heart transplant when there is no sign of disease, failure, or injury to the one they were born with? We must take this understanding and go on the offensive with it. If we take the battle into the enemy's camp, he will be too preoccupied defending his own camp to have time to attack ours! If we take the approach that we'll use the sword defensively only, then we are inviting the enemy to attack us in our own homes!

Take the sword of the Spirit to the heart of an unsaved soul. Preach it on every occasion. Teach it to any who will listen and even to those who won't. Take everything that is preached and hold it against the truth of Scripture. Take nothing for granted.

> Now these Jews were more noble than those in Thessalonica; they received the word with all eagerness, examining the Scriptures daily to see if these things were so. Many of them therefore believed, with not a few Greek women of high standing as well as men.
>
> Acts 17:11

You may be a timid and peaceful individual by nature and, as such, avoid conflict whenever possible, but our enemy is a keen foe and is interested only in your destruction and as such must be met with deadly force and deadly weapons wielded by a soldier with a warrior's heart!

Understand this—if you intend to play at Christian warfare, your enemies certainly will not!

It is a fight to the death—your enemy will give you no quarter. If you do not kill your enemy, he will assuredly kill you! Do not be content in conquering the drunkenness in your own life but attack it wherever it may be found.

Be not satisfied with slaying the enemy in your own heart but take the battle to him and attack sin in every dark corner where it hides and thrives. If we as Christians had done a better job of taking this fight to the enemy instead of hiding from him over the centuries, Satan might not have infiltrated our churches, our families, and our homes as greatly as he has. Now, however, we must fight him where he stands. In our marriages, in our children, in our churches, and in our pulpits! Not to do so spells our own doom and that of our children as well.

The sword is not decorative, as many have used it for and, yes, still use it today.

Bibles sit unopened on coffee tables and bedside tables, covered in dust on bookshelves and in closets. It is not to be hung on a wall for decoration so that all the world could see our "holiness" as would a cheap decorative sword. Our sword is the finest weapon ever created and it would be a slap across Jesus' face for us to not use it accordingly. It is not to be sheathed in opinion, criticism, and faulty doctrine as practiced by the Pharisees of old and Pharisees behind pulpits today. No, the sword is to be drawn, sharp, and firmly in our grasp, ready to parry blows with Satan at a moment's notice!

Is there a book, a chapter, or even a single verse that has not fallen under your eye? Shame on us all, for this, is where the blade is dullest! Sharpen it while there is still time! Read the Bible through, starting today so that no part of the sword would succumb to the blows of the enemy!

Start in your own home, your own heart, and slay the enemies within. Only then will you see clearly enough to remove the splinter from your brother's eye. How can we win a war on foreign soil when the enemy is camped in the capital of our heart!

Take the Sword with a purpose—To Stand. If you doubt, use the sword to kill that doubt with the truth of the word. If you fear, use the sword to kill that fear with the assurance of the word. Split the whole of every temptation, doubt, fear, etc. across the rapier of God's word!

CHAPTER 17

Prayer

We as Christians are commanded by God to pray.

Pray Without Ceasing.

1 Thessalonians 5:17

The Lord is at hand do not be anxious about anything, but in everything by prayer and supplication with thanksgiving let your requests be made known to God.

Philippians 4:6

First of all, then, I urge that supplications, prayers, intercessions, and thanksgivings be made for all people.

1 Timothy 2:1

Praying at all times in the Spirit, with all prayer and supplication. To that end keep alert with all perseverance, making supplication for all the saints, and also for me, that words may be given to me in opening my mouth boldly to proclaim the mystery of the gospel.

Ephesians 6:18-19

Moreover, as for me, far be it from me that I should sin against the Lord by ceasing to pray for you, and I will instruct you in the good and the right way.

1 Samuel 12:23

The Christ in my Cancer

We as Christians should all have an inherent desire to be as skilled in the "art" of prayer.

> Is anyone among you suffering? Let him pray. Is anyone cheerful? Let him sing praise. Is anyone among you sick? Let him call for the elders of the church, and let them pray over him, anointing him with oil in the name of the Lord. And the prayer of faith will save the one who is sick, and the Lord will raise him up. And if he has committed sins, he will be forgiven. Therefore, confess your sins to one another and pray for one another, that you may be healed. The prayer of a righteous person has great power as it is working. Elijah was a man with a nature like ours, and he prayed fervently that it might not rain, and for three years and six months it did not rain on the earth. Then he prayed again, and heaven gave rain, and the earth bore its fruit.
>
> James 5:13-18

We as Christians have been taught by Jesus Himself how to pray.

> "And when you pray, you must not be like the hypocrites. For they love to stand and pray in the synagogues and at the street corners, that they may be seen by others. Truly, I say to you, they have received their reward. But when you pray, go into your room and shut the door and pray to your Father who is in secret. And your Father who sees in secret will reward you. And when you pray, do not heap up empty phrases as the Gentiles do, for they think that they will be heard for their many words. Do not be like them, for your Father knows what you need before you ask him. Pray then like this: 'Our Father in heaven, hallowed be your name. Your kingdom come, your will be done, on earth as it is in heaven. Give us this day our daily bread, and forgive us our debts, as we also have

Prayer

forgiven our debtors. And lead us not into temptation but deliver us from evil.'"

"For if you forgive others their trespasses, your heavenly Father will also forgive you, but if you do not forgive others their trespasses, neither will your Father forgive your trespasses."

Matthew 6:5-15

How then should we pray?

And when you pray, you must not be like the hypocrites. For they love to stand and pray in the synagogues and at the street corners, so that they may be seen by others. Truly, I say to you, they have received their reward.

> Webster's Dictionary defines a Hypocrite as "a person who puts on a false appearance of virtue or religion."[17]

The Pharisees probably took care that the hour fixed for prayer should overtake them at a cross-road or the corner of a street, to afford them the desired opportunity of performing their devotions in the most public places. Their posture during these "public" prayers was often conspicuous as well. They would face the Temple (the most holy spot in Judaism) and would stand erect and still, many times kneeling or even laying prostrate to display their level of devotion.

Does God hear every prayer?

You ask and do not receive, because you ask amiss that you may spend it on your pleasures.

James 4:3

---

17 Webster's Dictionary: https://www.merriam-webster.com/dictionary/ Viewed October 11, 2022

The Christ in my Cancer

According to Scripture, God does not answer the prayers of those:

With iniquity in their hearts

> If I regard iniquity in my heart, the Lord will not hear.
>
> Psalm 66:18

Who remains in sin?

> But your iniquities have separated you from your God; And your sins have hidden His face from you, So that He will not hear.
>
> Isaiah 59:2

> Now we know that God does not hear sinners; but if anyone is a worshiper of God and does His will, He hears him.
>
> John 9:31

Who is offering unworthy service to God?

> You are offering polluted food upon my altar. But you say, "How have we polluted you?" By saying that the Lord's table may be despised. When you offer blind animals in sacrifice, is that not evil? And when you offer those that are lame or sick, is that not evil? Present that to your governor; will he accept you or show you favor? says the Lord of hosts.
>
> Malachi 1:7-8

Who forsakes God?

> Thus says the Lord concerning this people: "They have loved to wander; thus, they have not restrained their feet; therefore the Lord does not accept them; now he will remember their iniquity and punish their sins." The Lord said to me: "Do not pray for the welfare of this people. Though they fast, I will not hear their cry, and though

they offer burnt offering and grain offering, I will not accept them. But I will consume them by the sword, by famine, and by pestilence.

Jeremiah 14:10-12

Who rejects God's call?

Because I have called and you refused to listen, have stretched out my hand and no one has heeded, because you have ignored all my counsel and would have none of my reproof, I also will laugh at your calamity; I will mock when terror strikes you, when terror strikes you like a storm and your calamity comes like a whirlwind, when distress and anguish come upon you. Then they will call upon me, but I will not answer; they will seek me diligently but will not find me.

Proverbs 1:24-28

Who will not heed God's Law?

One who turns away his ear from hearing the law, even his prayer is an abomination.

Proverbs 28:9

But they refused to heed, shrugged their shoulders, and stopped their ears so that they could not hear. Yes, they made their hearts like flint, refusing to hear the law and the words which the Lord of hosts had sent by His Spirit through the former prophets. Thus great wrath came from the Lord of hosts. Therefore, it happened, that just as He proclaimed and they would not hear, so they called out and I would not listen," says the Lord of hosts.

Zechariah 7:11-13

Who turns a deaf ear to the cry of the poor?

> Whoever shuts his ears to the cry of the poor, Will also cry himself and not be heard.
>
> Proverbs 21:13

Who are violent?

> When you spread out your hands, I will hide My eyes from you; Even though you make many prayers, I will not hear. Your hands are full of blood.
>
> Isaiah 1:15

> but your iniquities have made a separation between you and your God, and your sins have hidden his face from you so that he does not hear. For your hands are defiled with blood and your fingers with iniquity; your lips have spoken lies; your tongue mutters wickedness.
>
> Isaiah 59:2-3

Who worships idols?

> Therefore, thus says the Lord: "Behold, I will surely bring calamity on them which they will not be able to escape; and though they cry out to Me, I will not listen to them. Then the cities of Judah and the inhabitants of Jerusalem will go and cry out to the gods to whom they offer incense, but they will not save them at all in the time of their trouble. For according to the number of your cities were your gods, O Judah; and according to the number of the streets of Jerusalem you have set up altars to that shameful thing, altars to burn incense to Baal. So do not pray for this people or lift up a cry or prayer for them; for I will not hear them in the time that they cry out to Me because of their trouble."
>
> Jeremiah 11:11-14

Prayer

Who has no faith?

But let him ask in faith, with no doubting, for he who doubts is like a wave of the sea driven and tossed by the wind. For let not that man suppose that he will receive anything from the Lord.

James 1:6-7

Who lives in hypocrisy?

"Beware of the leaven of the Pharisees, which is hypocrisy"

Luke 12:1

Who are proud?

God resists the proud, but gives grace to the humble.

James 4:6

Who are self-righteous?

"The Pharisee stood and prayed thus with himself, God, I thank You that I am not like other men—extortioners, unjust, adulterers, or even as this tax collector. I fast twice a week; I give tithes of all that I possess. And the tax collector, standing afar off, would not so much as raise his eyes to heaven, but beat his breast, saying, God, be merciful to me a sinner! I tell you, this man went down to his house justified rather than the other; for everyone who exalts himself will be humbled, and he who humbles himself will be exalted"

Luke 18:11-14

Who mistreats God's people?

You have also given me the necks of my enemies, So that I destroyed those who hated me. They cried out, but there was none to save; Even to the Lord, but He did not answer them.

Psalm 18:40-41

> You who hate good and love evil; Who strip the skin from My people, And the flesh from their bones; Who also eat the flesh of My people, Flay their skin from them, Break their bones, And chop them in pieces, Like meat for the pot, Like flesh in the caldron. Then they will cry to the Lord, But He will not hear them; He will even hide His face from them at that time, Because they have been evil in their deeds.
>
> Micah 3:2-4

Does God hear every prayer? It would appear that He does not.

Effective prayer—the prayers that God does hear

2 Chronicles 6:12-42 allows us to see Solomon's prayer of dedication of the temple to God which is an extremely strong example of effective and meaningful prayer.

Nehemiah chapter 9 also gives an example of a beautiful public prayer. You see it is not the location of the prayer but the attitude of the heart behind the prayer that is what is important.

As Christ taught us to pray . . .

> **Heidelberg Q120 Why has Christ commanded us to address God as "Our Father"?**
>
> That immediately, in the very beginning of our prayer, he might excite in us a childlike reverence for, and confidence in God, which are the foundation of our prayer: namely, that God is become our Father in Christ, and will much less deny us what we ask of him in true faith, than our parents will refuse us earthly things.[18]

---

18 *Heidelberg Catechism*. Westminster Theological Seminary. (n.d.) https://students.wts.edu/resources/creeds/heidelberg.html Viewed October 11, 2022

Prayer

"Or what man is there of you, whom if his son ask bread, will he give him a stone? Or if he ask a fish, will he give him a serpent. If ye then, being evil, know how to give good gifts unto your children, how much more shall your Father which is in heaven give good things to them that ask him?"

Matthew 7:9-11

"If a son shall ask bread of any of you that is a father, will he give him a stone? or if he ask a fish, will he for a fish give him a serpent?" "Or if he shall ask an egg, will he offer him a scorpion?" "If ye then, being evil, know how to give good gifts unto your children: how much more shall your heavenly Father give the Holy Spirit to them that ask him?"

Luke 11:11-13

> **Heidelberg Q121 Why did Christ add the words "Who art In Heaven"?**
>
> Lest we should form any earthly conceptions of God's heavenly majesty, and that we may expect from his almighty power all things necessary for soul and body.[19]

Am I a God at hand, saith the LORD, and not a God afar off? Can any hide himself in secret places that I shall not see him? saith the LORD. Do not I fill heaven and earth? saith the LORD?

Jeremiah 23:23-24

---

19 *Heidelberg Catechism*. Westminster Theological Seminary. (n.d.) https://students.wts.edu/resources/creeds/heidelberg.html Viewed October 11, 2022

God that made the world and all things therein, seeing that he is Lord of heaven and earth, dwelleth not in temples made with hands; Neither is worshipped with men's hands, as though he needed anything, seeing he giveth to all life, and breath, and all things? That they should seek the Lord, if haply they might feel after him, and find him, though he be not far from every one of us.

Acts 17:24-27

For there is no difference between the Jew and the Greek: for the same Lord over all is rich unto all that call upon him.

Romans 10:12

> **Heidelberg Q122 Which is the first petition to the Lord?**
>
> "Hallowed be thy name"; that is, grant us, first, rightly to know thee, and to sanctify, glorify and praise thee, in all thy works, in which thy power, wisdom, goodness, justice, mercy and truth, are clearly displayed; and further also, that we may so order and direct our whole lives, our thoughts, words and actions, that thy name may never be blasphemed, but rather honored and praised on our account.[20]

that they know you the only true God, and Jesus Christ whom you have sent.

John 17:3

And Mary said, My soul doth magnify the Lord. And my spirit hath rejoiced in God my Savior.

Luke 1:46-47

---

[20] *Heidelberg Catechism.* Westminster Theological Seminary. (n.d.) https://students.wts.edu/resources/creeds/heidelberg.html Viewed October 11, 2022

Prayer

But let him that glory in this, that he understand and know me, that I am the LORD which exercise lovingkindness, judgment, and righteousness, in the earth: for in these things I delight, saith the LORD.

Jeremiah 9:24

But this shall be the covenant that I will make with the house of Israel; After those days, saith the LORD, I will put my law in their inward parts, and write it in their hearts; and will be their God, and they shall be my people. And they shall teach no more every man his neighbor, and every man his brother, saying, Know the LORD: for they shall all know me, from the least of them unto the greatest of them, saith the LORD: for I will forgive their iniquity, and I will remember their sin no more?

Jeremiah 31:33-34

And Jesus answered and said unto him, "Blessed art thou, Simon Bar-Jonah! for flesh and blood hath not revealed it unto thee, but my Father which is in heaven."

Matthew 16:17

If any of you lack wisdom, let him ask of God, that giveth to all men liberally, and upbraided not; and it shall be given him.

James 1:5

Thy word is a lamp unto my feet, and a light unto my path. Righteous art thou, O LORD, and upright are thy judgments.

Psalm 119:105, 137

Let my mouth be filled with thy praise and thy honor all day.

Psalm 71:8

The Christ in my Cancer

O the depth of the riches both of the wisdom and knowledge of God! how unsearchable are his judgments, and his ways past finding out! For whom hath known the mind of the Lord? or who hath been his counselor? Or who hath first given to him, and it shall be recompensed unto him again? For of him, and through him, and to him, are all things: to whom be glory forever. Amen.

Romans 11:33-36

Blessed be the Lord God of Israel; for he hath visited and redeemed his people, and hath raised up a horn of salvation for us in the house of his servant David;

Luke 1:68-69

Not unto us, O LORD, not unto us, but unto thy name give glory, for thy mercy, and for thy truth's sake.

Psalm 115:1

Heidelberg Q123 What is the second petition to the Lord?

"Thy kingdom come"; that is, rule us so by thy word and Spirit, that we may submit ourselves more and more to thee; preserve and increase thy church; destroy the works of the devil, and all violence which would exalt itself against thee; and also, all wicked counsels devised against thy holy word; till the full perfection of thy kingdom take place, wherein thou shalt be all in all.[21]

"But seek ye first the kingdom of God, and his righteousness; and all these things shall be added unto you."

Matthew 6:33

---

21 *Heidelberg Catechism.* Westminster Theological Seminary. (n.d.) https://students.wts.edu/resources/creeds/heidelberg.html Viewed October 11, 2022

Prayer

O that my ways were directed to keep thy statutes!

Psalm 119:5

Teach me to do thy will; for thou art my God: thy spirit is good; lead me into the land of uprightness.

Psalm 143:10

Do good in thy good pleasure unto Zion: build thou the walls of Jerusalem.

Psalm 51:18

Pray for the peace of Jerusalem: they shall prosper that love thee. Peace be within thy walls, and prosperity within thy palaces. For my brethren and companions' sakes, I will now say, Peace be within thee. Because of the house of the LORD our God I will seek thy good.

Psalm 122:6-9

He that commits sin is of the devil; for the devil sins from the beginning. For this purpose, the Son of God was manifested, that he might destroy the works of the devil.

1 John 3:8

And the God of peace shall bruise Satan under your feet shortly. The grace of our Lord Jesus Christ be with you. Amen.

Romans 16:20

And the Spirit and the bride say, Come. And let him that hears say, Come. And let him that is athirst come. And whosoever will, let him take the water of life freely. He which testifies these things saith, Surely, I come quickly. Amen. Even so, come, Lord Jesus.

Revelation 22:17, 20

For we know that the whole creation groans and travails in pain together until now. And not only they, but ourselves also, which have the first fruits of the Spirit, even we ourselves groan within ourselves, waiting for the adoption, to wit, the redemption of our body.

> Romans 8:22-23

And when all things shall be subdued unto him, then shall the Son also himself be subject unto him that put all things under him, that God may be all in all.

> 1 Corinthians 15:28

Brethren, let every man, wherein he is called, therein abide with God

> 1 Corinthians 7:24

Bless the LORD, ye his angels, that excel in strength, that do his commandments, hearkening unto the voice of his word" Bless ye the LORD, all ye his hosts; ye ministers of his, that do his pleasure.

> Psalm' 103:20-21

Heidelberg Q125 What is the fourth petition to the Lord?

"Give us this day our daily bread"; that is, be pleased to provide us with all things necessary for the body, that we may thereby acknowledge thee to be the only fountain of all good, and that neither our care nor industry, nor even thy gifts, can profit us without thy blessing; and therefore that we may withdraw our trust from all creatures, and place it alone in thee.[22]

---

22 *Heidelberg Catechism.* Westminster Theological Seminary. (n.d.) https://students.wts.edu/resources/creeds/heidelberg.html Viewed October 11, 2022

Prayer

These wait all upon thee; that thou may give them their meat in due season. That thou give them they gather: thou open thy hand, they are filled with good.

Psalm 104:27-28

> **Heidelberg Q124 What is the third petition to the Lord?**
>
> "Thy will be done on earth as it is in heaven"; that is, grant that we and all men may renounce our own will, and without murmuring obey thy will, which is only good; that everyone may attend to, and perform the duties of his station and calling, as willingly and faithfully as the angels do in heaven.[23]

"Then said Jesus unto his disciples, If any man will come after me, let him deny himself, and take up his cross, and follow me."

Matthew 16:24

For the grace of God that brings salvation hath appeared to all men, teaching us that, denying ungodliness and worldly lusts, we should live soberly, righteously, and godly, in this present world;

Titus 2:11-12

Saying, Father, if thou be willing, remove this cup from me: nevertheless, not my will, but thy, be done.

Luke 22:42

Proving what is acceptable unto the Lord.

Ephesians 5:10

---

23 *Heidelberg Catechism*. Westminster Theological Seminary. (n.d.) https://students.wts.edu/resources/creeds/heidelberg.html Viewed October 11, 2022

The Christ in my Cancer

And be not conformed to this world: but be ye transformed by the renewing of your mind, that ye may prove what is that good, and acceptable, and perfect, will of God.

Romans 12:2

The eyes of all wait upon thee; and thou give them their meat in due season. Thou open thy hand and satisfy the desire of every living thing.

Psalm 145:15-16

"Therefore, I say unto you, Take no thought for your life, what ye shall eat, or what ye shall drink; nor yet for your body, what ye shall put on. Is not the life more than meat, and the body than raiment?" Behold the fowls of the air: for they sow not, neither do they reap, nor gather into barns; yet your heavenly Father feed them. Are ye not much better than they?"

Matthew 6:25-26

God hath spoken once; twice have I heard this; that power belongs unto God.

Psalm 62:11

Every good gift and every perfect gift is from above, and cometh down from the Father of lights, with whom is no variableness, neither shadow of turning.

James 1:17

And he humbled thee, and suffered thee to hunger, and fed thee with manna, which thou knew not, neither did thy fathers know; that he might make thee know that man doth not live by bread only, but by every word that proceed out of the mouth of the LORD doth man live.

Deuteronomy 8:3

Prayer

Nevertheless he left not himself without witness, in that he did good, and gave us rain from heaven, and fruitful seasons, filling our hearts with food and gladness.

Acts 14:17

That they should seek the Lord, if haply they might feel after him, and find him, though he be not far from every one of us:

Acts 17:27

For in him we live, and move, and have our being; as certain also of your own poets have said, For we are also his offspring.

Acts 27:18;

Therefore, my beloved brethren, be ye steadfast, un-moveable, always abounding in the work of the Lord, forasmuch as ye know that your labor is not in vain in the Lord.

1 Corinthians 15:58

Trust in the LORD, and do good; so shalt thou dwell in the land, and verily thou shalt be fed." Delight thyself also in the LORD; and he shall give thee the desires of thy heart. Commit thy way unto the LORD; trust also in him; and he shall bring it to pass. A little that a righteous man hath is better than the riches of many wicked.

Psalm 37:3-5, 16

Except the LORD build the house, they labor in vain that build it: except the LORD keep the city, the watchman wakes but in vain. It is vain for you to rise up early, to sit up late, to eat the bread of sorrows: for so he giveth his beloved sleep.

Psalm 127:1-2

But thou, O God, shalt bring them down into the pit of destruction: bloody and deceitful men shall not live out half their days; but I will trust in thee.

Psalm 55:23

Thus, saith the LORD; "Cursed be the man that trusts in man, and makes flesh his arm, and whose heart departs from the LORD. Blessed is the man that trusts in the LORD, and whose hope the LORD is."

Jeremiah 17:5, 7

> **Heidelberg Q126 What is the fifth petition to the Lord?**
>
> "And forgive us our debts as we forgive our debtors"; that is, be pleased for the sake of Christ's blood, not to impute to us poor sinners, our transgressions, nor that depravity, which always cleaves to us; even as we feel this evidence of thy grace in us, that it is our firm resolution from the heart to forgive our neighbor.[23]

There is therefore now no condemnation to them which are in Christ Jesus, who walk not after the flesh, but after the Spirit.

Romans 8:1

My little children, these things write I unto you, that ye sin not. And if any man sin, we have an advocate with the Father, Jesus Christ the righteous: And he is the propitiation for our sins: and not for ours only, but also for the sins of the whole world.

1 John 2:1-2

---

[23] *Heidelberg Catechism.* Westminster Theological Seminary. (n.d.) https://students.wts.edu/resources/creeds/heidelberg.html Viewed October 11, 2022

Prayer

And enter not into judgment with thy servant: for in thy sight shall no man living be justified.

Psalm 143:2

Have mercy upon me, O God, according to thy lovingkindness: according unto the multitude of thy tender mercies blot out my transgressions. Wash me thoroughly from mine iniquity, and cleanse me from my sin. For I acknowledge my transgressions: and my sin is ever before me. Against thee, thee only, have I sinned, and done this evil in thy sight: that thou might be justified when thou speak, and be clear when thou judge Behold, I was shaped in iniquity; and in sin did my mother conceive me. Behold, thou desire truth in the inward parts: and in the hidden part thou shalt make me to know wisdom. urge me with hyssop, and I shall be clean: wash me, and I shall be whiter than snow.

Psalm 51:1-7

"For if ye forgive men their trespasses, your heavenly Father will also forgive you:" But if ye forgive not men their trespasses, neither will your Father forgive your trespasses."

Matthew 6:14-15

Heidelberg Q127 What is the sixth petition to the Lord?

"And lead us not into temptation, but deliver us from evil"; that is, since we are so weak in ourselves, that we cannot stand a moment; and besides this, since our mortal enemies, the devil, the world, and our own flesh cease not to assault us, do thou, therefore, preserve and strengthen us by the power of thy Holy Spirit, that we may not be overcome in this spiritual warfare, but constantly and strenuously may resist our foes, till at last, we obtain a complete victory.[24]

---

24 *Heidelberg Catechism.* Westminster Theological Seminary. (n.d.) https://students.wts.edu/resources/creeds/heidelberg.html Viewed October 11, 2022

The Christ in my Cancer

"I am the vine, ye are the branches: He that abides in me, and I in him, the same brings forth much fruit: for without me ye can do nothing."

John 15:5

For he knows our frame; he remembers that we are dust.

Psalm 103:14

Be sober, be vigilant; because your adversary the devil, as a roaring lion, walking about, seeking whom he may devour:

1 Peter 5:8

For we wrestle not against flesh and blood, but against principalities, against powers, against the rulers of the darkness of this world, against spiritual wickedness in high places.

Ephesians 6:12

"If ye were of the world, the world would love his own: but because ye are not of the world, but I have chosen you out of the world, therefore the world hates you."

John 15:19

But I see another law in my members, warring against the law of my mind, and bringing me into captivity to the law of sin which is in my members.

Romans 7:23

For the flesh lusts against the Spirit, and the Spirit against the flesh: and these are contrary the one to the other: so that ye cannot do the things that ye would.

Galatians 5:17

"Watch and pray, that ye enter not into temptation: the spirit indeed is willing, but the flesh is weak."

Matthew 26:41

Prayer

"Take ye heed, watch and pray: for ye know not when time is."

Mark 13:33

To the end he may establish your hearts un-blamable in holiness before God, even our Father, at the coming of our Lord Jesus Christ with all his saints.

1 Thessalonians 3:13

And the very God of peace sanctify you wholly; and I pray God your whole spirit and soul and body be preserved blameless unto the coming of our Lord Jesus Christ.

1 Thessalonians 5:23

Heidelberg Q128 How do we conclude the prayer?

"For thine is the kingdom, and the power, and the glory, forever"; that is, all these we ask of thee, because thou, being our King and almighty, art willing and able to give us all good; and all this we pray for, that thereby not we, but thy holy name, may be glorified forever.[25]

For the scripture saith, Whosoever believeth on him shall not be ashamed For there is no difference between the Jew and the Greek: for the same Lord over all is rich unto all that call upon him.

Romans 10:11-12

The Lord knows how to deliver the godly out of temptations, and to reserve the unjust unto the day of judgment to be punished:

2 Peter 2:9

---

25 *Heidelberg Catechism*. Westminster Theological Seminary. (n.d.) https://students.wts.edu/resources/creeds/heidelberg.html Viewed October 11, 2022

The Christ in my Cancer

"And whatsoever ye shall ask in my name, that will I do, that the Father may be glorified in the Son."

John 14:13

And I will cleanse them from all their iniquity, whereby they have sinned against me; and I will pardon all their iniquities, whereby they have sinned, and whereby they have transgressed against me. And it shall be to me a name of joy, a praise and an honor before all the nations of the earth, which shall hear all the good that I do unto them: and they shall fear and tremble for all the goodness and for all the prosperity that I procure unto it.

Jeremiah 33:8-9

Not unto us, O LORD, not unto us, but unto thy name give glory, for thy mercy, and for thy truth's sake.

Psalm 115:1

Heidelberg Q129 What does the word "Amen" signify?

"Amen" signifies, it shall truly and certainly be: for my prayer is more assuredly heard of God than I feel in my heart that I desire these things of him.[26]

or all the promises of God in him are yea, and in him Amen, unto the glory of God by us.

2 Corinthians 1:20

If we believe not, yet he abides faithful: he cannot deny himself.

2 Timothy 2:13

---

26 *Heidelberg Catechism*. Westminster Theological Seminary. (n.d.) https://students.wts.edu/resources/creeds/heidelberg.html Viewed October 11, 2022

Prayer

Learn and know how to pray in a manner that not only pleases God but also does not offend Him.

Our Father who art in heaven:

We are to approach the cross in humility, recognizing that we are entering into the throne room of the Creator of the Universe.

Hallowed be Thy name:

Our prayers should begin with praise to our Lord, acknowledging His supremacy and authority over our lives. This realization helps prepare our hearts as well to enter His Holy presence.

Your kingdom come:

We need to acknowledge that God does indeed have the plan to restore His Holy Kingdom here on earth and that we are to be the key players in the accomplishment of His will in this.

Your will be done on earth as [it is] in heaven:

In this, we are instructed to pray that He prepares us to fully submit ourselves to His will. We are to understand that God is in complete control of every situation, that He reigns in Heaven, that there is none above Him, and that nothing happens of which He is not aware. We need to realize that God ordains our lives and sets our paths so that we might be used to complete the fulfillment of His will here on earth.

Give us this day our daily bread:

This involves a changing of the heart for most of us. It means that we are to ask God to help us trust Him for our every need. He desires that we become servants who are willing and able to trust Him with our needs for today and allow Him to take care of the things that we will need tomorrow.

And forgive us our debts, As we forgive our debtors:

Ask God to forgive you of your sins against Him. He sent His Son Jesus Christ so that He could do just that if only we would accept that Jesus paid the penalty for our guilt. However, there is a caveat here. He will only forgive us of our sins if we first forgive those with whom we hold a grudge. Pray that God would show you those areas and people in your life that He requires you to forgive. Without this forgiveness, God can never forgive you.

And do not lead us into temptation, but deliver us from the evil one:

Pray for divine protection over yourself and your loved ones that God would keep the enemy (Satan) away from you. 1 Peter 5:8 warns us that, "Satan walks about like a roaring lion seeking whom he may devour." Pray continuously that God would keep Satan and his attacks from entering your life.

For Yours is the kingdom and the power and the glory forever, Amen:

> Just as we are instructed to enter into prayer with praise, we are also instructed to close our prayers with praise and acknowledgment of His sovereignty.

In short, Jesus gives us the key components of prayer as follows; Acknowledge the absolute authority of God. Praise and worship Him. Seek the fulfillment of His will. Ask for your basic needs while surrendering everything else to his plans. Seek forgiveness as well as the ability to forgive. Ask for divine protection. Close with praise and submission.

We are to pray in solitude with God. We are not to wear our faith on our sleeves as many do, trying to impress others with their pious attitudes, and holy rhetoric. We are to seek the presence of the Almighty God Himself when we pray. It sets a condition of the heart wherein we prepare ourselves to enter into God's divine presence and become receptive to the hearing of His voice. We are to commune with God during our prayers, letting His spirit wash over us as we dwell in His midst. In Matthew 26:36 Jesus tells His disciples; "Sit here while I go and pray over there". Jesus separated Himself from the others He was with (even His disciples) and went alone to pray and commune with His Father. He came back to the disciples during His prayers and twice again demonstrates the principle of praying alone with God in Matthew 26:42 and 44.

Do not rely on fancy words when you pray or think that you cannot express your needs to God. He understands your needs even before you approach His throne in prayer. Luke 12:7 tells us that God knows the exact number of hairs on your head at any given time. Did you ever lose hair? God is aware of each and every hair that we lose. How then can we think that He does not know our prayers and our needs unless we tell them to Him? Remember—prayer is about communing with God, basking in His presence, not about complaining to Him or asking for favors from Him.

Father God—I acknowledge your sovereignty over my life and the world around me. You are the Creator of the universe, and glorious in every aspect. You are worthy of all praise and worship. I come humbly before your throne in a spirit of submission, seeking your will for my life. Father show me the plan you have for my life and give me your strength so that I may follow it. Provide the things that only You know I need to get through this day and help me to allow you to direct everything else. Show me, Lord, those whom I have yet to forgive so that You in turn can then forgive me through Jesus. Lord, I ask that you provide for the protection of myself, my family, and my friends as we seek to follow your lead. Keep the attacks of the enemy at bay. Father, I thank you for loving me enough to hear this prayer, and I thank you in advance for an answer to my prayer. Glorify yourself through each one reading this today, Lord, and instruct their hearts in the way that you would have them go. In Jesus' name, Amen.

www.ingramcontent.com/pod-product-compliance
Lightning Source LLC
Chambersburg PA
CBHW050106170426
43198CB00014B/2474